Ethics in Direct Sales
The Rising of a Gold Standard 3.0 Life!

Kevin D. McNabb

Ethics in Direct Sales – The Rising of a Gold Standard 3.0 Life™

Project editor – Roy Thomas

Designed by Shauna Rae of Shauna Rae Design. www.ShaunaRae.ca

ISBN: 1492357049

ISBN-13: 978-1492357049

DEDICATION

I would like to dedicate this book to my Mom!

She was the one throughout my schooling that sat at the dinner table and helped me with my homework and grilled me on various subjects.

I was not the strongest student in school, however because of my Mom, I wasn't the weakest either.

She taught me that even though some things may seem difficult at first, with a little hard work, the personal satisfaction you receive from accomplishing that task is so rewarding. For this I thank her.

I know Mom that at times you just sat there and shook your head and probably wondered whether or not I would amount to anything or achieve anything. I hope now you see that it was worth it.

I Love You!

Thanks for all you have done.

CONTENTS

Kevin D. McNabb

ACKNOWLEDGMENTS

First of all I would like to thank and acknowledge all of the giants in the Direct Selling Profession that came before me and allowed me to walk in their footsteps through this global minefield.

Rocky, wherever you are out there, thank you for first introducing me to the world of Direct Selling.

I would like to thank Dr. Yvonne Haas, my physician who has helped me immensely the past four years.

To my surgeon, Dr. Paul Bernicke, I appreciate all that you have done, and I especially appreciate the steady hand on the scalpel.

A special thanks to Shauna Rae of Shauna Rae Designs for the artwork on the cover. Your friendship and creativity are inspiring.

A special thanks to Roy Thomas my friend and the individual who edited this book. I can't tell you how much I appreciate you taking on this project and helping me transform this content into something that makes sense.

My unconditional love to my wife and daughter for being so very patient during the writing of this book. It may have felt at times like it was perhaps not going to get done, yet here we are.

CHAPTER 1

THE REASON WHY I AM THE IDEAL PERSON TO WRITE THIS BOOK

Dear Reader,

Thank you for taking the time to check out my new book, **"Ethics in Direct Sales – Introduction to a Gold Standard 3.0 Life!"**

Often when I pick up a book that has caught my eye, I immediately look at the name of the author to see if I happen to be familiar with their work.

The real question inside is, *"Why is this person writing this book, and why should I listen to them?"*

So, allow me to answer that question up front.

At the time of writing this book I am celebrating my 48th year on our wonderful planet and my 29th year in the direct selling industry.

During that time I probably have reached *"Hall-of-Fame"* status on the number of bad decisions that I have made.

I have made bad decisions in my personal life, with family, with friends, in my relationships, in my career and yes, in my involvement within the Direct Selling Profession.

Have I had questionable ethics in my past, absolutely! Has it happened often? No, but enough that it raised a few eyebrows.

So why am I telling you this?

We all make mistakes, we all make bad decisions, and to some extent, we all make questionably bad ethical decisions.

The only differences between others and me are the following:

I am admitting to my questionable ethical decisions in the past,

I have realigned my priorities with my values to avoid these traps in the future,

I am identifying a problem within our profession,

I am offering a sound solution to this problem.

This is why I believe that I offer not only a unique perspective on the subject of "*ethics*," but I am also distinctive in that I am offering a solution to a problem.

Remember, when Homeland Security or Global security firms are testing their services, they hire people who are used to breaking into these systems to perform the test.

Computer firms hire computer hackers; vault companies hire safe crackers, etc...

If it makes it easier, think of me as offering my services to the subject of "*ethics*."

Enjoy the Read!

CHAPTER 2
WHAT EXACTLY IS DIRECT SELLING?

It is humorous to talk with family or friends after 29 years in the Direct Selling Profession and find out that most still don't understand what it is that I do.

Therefore, just before we begin the journey through this book, allow us to all get on the same page and understand what the Direct Selling Profession really is.

Perhaps we can begin by adopting the following premise, rather than looking at direct selling as an industry, my professional recommendation would be to view it as a profession. Why? I believe that the two are fundamentally different. An industry is the ownership and management of companies, factories, etc... Whereas a profession is a body of persons engaged in an occupation or calling. You see, one focuses on bricks and mortar and the other on people.

Direct selling is the selling connected with a consumer product or service, person-to-person, fully removed from a fixed retail store location, promoted by means of independent sales representatives that happen to be characteristically also referred to as consultants, distributors or other titles. Direct sellers are definitely not employees of any direct selling company.

They are independent contractors who actually promote and sell the products or services of a direct selling organization in return for a commission (percentage) on those sales.

Product and Service Orders are generally placed in person or via the consultant's Web site. Occasionally the telephone can be used to place orders or reorders, however only about 12% of sales occur in this manner. Home shopping parties are definitely the most widely recognized product sales method, where friends, family members or acquaintances gather for a couple of hours to educate themselves about or sample a selection of products or services. Nevertheless, the majority (about 70%) of the direct selling industry's sales truly take place utilizing a one-to-one method where one direct seller may present the products or services to a single consumer.

Virtually any product or service is available for purchase through direct selling somewhere on the planet. Many individuals think about cosmetics, wellness products and home décor as products that are frequently sold through direct sales, however additionally there are numerous other product categories such as kitchen products, jewelry, clothing, organic gardening supplies, spa products, scrapbooking supplies, rubber stamps and much, much more.

Direct selling really should not be mistaken for some other type of sales that occur removed from a fixed retail location such as magazine sales, home repair services, telemarketing, wholesaling, real estate sales, or *"work-from-home"* businesses such as envelope stuffing or product assembly. [i]

CHAPTER 3
WHY I WROTE THIS BOOK

For the past 29 years I have been a member of the Direct Selling Profession, and I have witnessed some extraordinary things.

I have witnessed incredible acts of kindness and love that unfortunately went uncelebrated, and I have also witnessed criminal acts that went unpunished.

At this point it really is important that you just do not get the wrong impression. I love being a part of the Direct Selling Profession. As a matter of fact I consider myself to be a Direct Selling Professional; nevertheless, there are numerous areas within the profession that definitely need cleaning.

PART 1 - MY EXPERIENCES WITH UNETHICAL PRACTICES WITH THE DIRECT SELLING PROFESSION

I am a direct seller and this is my story... (Key music from "*Law & Order*")

In 1985, I made a decision to split my time and attempt to straddle between my corporate day job and building a direct selling business.

In hindsight, I reckon that I was fortunate, simply because within the first week of becoming a member of my chosen direct selling company, I had the opportunity to witness the "*real*" side of my sponsor.

It started when I was placing my first order. I fully understood the compensation plan, so I knew what it took to take full advantage of my monthly compensation. My sponsor sat down with me and we filled out the order form.

Now keep in mind, its 1985, thus making this a long time before direct shipments to our home became available, auto-ship, and any of those services that we take for granted now.

Back in those days (boy do I sound like my parents), individual distributor orders were collected by your up line and a massive bulk order was shipped to your up lines address and we had the pleasure of driving to pick it up.

No problem, right? Allow me to ask you a question. What city around the world does your sponsor live in?

I do believe that you're most likely beginning to see the problem at hand.

I lived in Toronto, Canada and my sponsor lived in Montreal, Canada which is approximately 5.5 hours by car one way.

So, back to the story... It's time to pick up my very first order.

I made arrangements with my sponsor to meet him and his wife at their home in Montreal on a particular Saturday morning. The arrangements we made were for 9:00a.m. They were not very flexible, they wanted to enjoy their free time that they felt they deserved.

That meant that I had to leave Toronto at 3:00a.m. To drive to Montreal (Nice!). It was September, so with luck, I should not have a problem, right?

Did I mention that Canada gets snow? Well, isn't it a little early for snow in September? You tell Mother Nature!

I leave early just in case and I make it on time. Now the reality of the situation unfolds.

My sponsor opens his garage and it is loaded full, I mean full of boxes. It takes us 2 hours to collect my order and it consists of 17 boxes of approximately 2'x2'x2'.

Big problem!

Forget the fact that I was driving a car, my sponsor hands me my invoice and asks me for a check. The total was $3,719.82? Holy $#%&!

I inform him that there must be some mistake, because my order was only for $276.23!

Now, here comes my first experience with unethical practices.

My sponsor proceeds to tell me that he increased my order, so that I would get a commission check in my first month. It was going to only be $8.02 but I could now tell people that I made money in my first month. Didn't seem to matter to him that my check for $8.02 was going to cost me $3,443.59!

So, before we get too far along, let me point out the first unethical practice.

Unethical Practice #1 - Changing Someone's Order without Their Permission

Let's get back to the story, shall we?

It goes without having to say that as I stood there I was a little miffed (put into an irritable mood, especially by an offending incident) to say the least.

We argue and I finally tell him that I was not going to take any of the products and under no conditions was I going to write him a check.

I got back in the car and drove the 5.5 hours back to Toronto.

A couple weeks later, I receive my credit card statement with the full charge of $3,719.82. I place a call to my sponsor to inquire what has happened and he tells me he will look into it as soon as they get back from a corporate trip that they won.

He proceeds to explain to me the benefits of the opportunity that I was already in, and whispers to me the amount of money that he and his wife were making and how I had made the right choice.

Unethical Practice #2 - Federal Trade Commission (FTC) Forbids the Disclosure of Earning Potential

Their "*corporate*" trip was for two weeks in the Caribbean, so he promised that he would look into my order and the billing problem as soon as they got back.

As soon as I got off the phone, I called the corporation and explained my dilemma. They told me that they would look into it and it should be just a few days.

Less than a day later, the corporation calls me back and says that they have gotten to the bottom of the problem.

You see, my sponsor and his wife charged the shipment to my credit card, and then they returned the entire product back to the corporation and received a $3,719.82 refund.

Allow me to explain.

Back in the day, as you achieved a certain rank within the company, you had to take care of all your distributors. Orders were called into you, you placed all the orders, the products was delivered to you, your distributors had to come and pick it up, and when any commissions were written, they did not come in your name, they came in your up lines' name and they wrote you a personal check.

You are probably wondering what happened to my sponsor and his wife, so let's go back and find out.

The week they were to return I started to call and leave messages (*yes there were answering machines back then*). One day, two days, first week, second week...

That's it; it's time to call the corporation again.

After being passed from one customer service representative to another, I finally am able to speak with the VP of Sales and Marketing.

I explain my situation and he takes down the name of my sponsor and promises to call me right back.

Later that afternoon, I receive a return call from the VP who is a bit perplexed (*I had to look that up*). He proceeds to tell me that my sponsor and his wife were not on a corporate trip that they earned, and also that they had only been in the business for 3 months.

After several weeks of going back and forth with the corporation, my $3,719.82 was finally returned.

What happened to my sponsor and his wife?

No one knows, they quit the business and I have never heard from them again.

That was probably the first time that I consciously thought of quitting. But I didn't.

A few years later, I was able to witness the ole "*commission check*" scam.

If you remember from earlier, all commissions were paid directly to a certain level of your up line.

My up line at the time had a fairly big down line, so when the monthly commission checks arrived, my up line would have to sit down with the commission reports and write individual personal checks to all their distributors. It was so complicated; it would have taken a firm like Arthur Anderson to figure it out correctly. (Whoops, perhaps Arthur Anderson was a bad example!)

Remember, back in the early 1990's we didn't have "*online*" access, so a master commission report would be sent to your up line only.

This was crazy for two reasons (probably more if I really thought about it):

As a distributor, we never knew where our down line stood from a monthly point's perspective until it was too late to make any last minute pushes to reach higher commission levels.

As an independent distributor, you never knew the amount of the commission check, until it was placed in your hand.

So, as I mentioned above, I received a commission check on this particular month that I was expecting to be quite substantial.

However, when my up line handed me my commission check, he said, *"What happened, I thought your numbers were much better than this?"*

I look down at the check and the amount showed less than half of what I was expecting.

I knew within a few dollars the expected amount since at this point I was talking with the corporation on a daily basis because my business was really growing.

We talked about the amount and my sponsor became quite offended when he felt that I was accusing him of short changing me. Now, I in no way implied that it was an intentional mistake, but once he had brought it up, I began to wonder.

For the whole remainder of the month, I worked with the corporation to rectify the discrepancy.

End result, the check was for the wrong amount. The reports were correct that my up line received. Several of their down line had contacted the corporation about commission check discrepancies.

Three weeks later, my up line quit. As far as I know, the corporation recouped their money, but my up line was never criminally charged, they were only banned for life. A few years later a promotional trip that I earned for organizational growth (I really did earn it), I ran into a senior executive in charge of sales and marketing and we discussed the situation.

As it turned out, my up line got them into some significant financial trouble and made an unethical decision to use other people's commissions to cover their losses.

In my opinion looking back, the problem was shared by both the corporation and my up line.

First of all, even thought we did not have the accounting and check writing services that we do now, the corporation should have set up a third party company to dispense all the checks via the mail.

I would like to have softened the language a bit, but at the end of the day, two people make a conscious decision to take money that didn't belong to them.

During the first 15 years of being part of the Direct Selling Profession, one of the stories that I used to hear (way too often unfortunately) was about how some of the leaders in our profession chose to buy their way to a certain level and recognition in the business.

Here is what I mean by "*buying*" their way. The majority of us understand that no commissions are earned unless products and services are purchased. However, the basic concept within direct selling is to build a team of a lot of people, personally consuming a small amount of their own products and services. It was never designed for a small amount of people to personally consume a lot of their own products and services.

I had an up line about three or four levels above me at the time purchasing significant amounts of products and services from their own business that would be next to impossible to personally consume in a month.

So what was their rationale for this unethical practice?

The corporation and the teams that were built within the corporation were fueled by recognition and money.

That shouldn't be a problem right?

Well, no it shouldn't unless you add people and ego to the mix.

My up line made the decision that rather that working and building and nurturing a team of distributors to grow exponentially, thus raising them up the compensation ladder; they had their own way of doing it.

First of all, long before they got into the business, they were pretty rich, so money shouldn't have been an issue.

Unethical Practice #3 - Theft

As their team was building beneath them, they would buy large amounts product each month, thus generating a healthy commission check, which would offset some of their losses. But eventually what happened was they achieved a very high level on the compensation ladder and were allowed to speak at major company functions.

I remember, sitting there listening to them speak from stage and talk about their close knit team and the roads they travelled and the sacrifices they made. Boy what a crock of &%$@!

So, who cares, they didn't hurt anybody, right?

Wrong.

They would teach this idea on tele-seminars to their entire organization.

I remember one of the first calls I was on, I had a majority of my organization, as well as new prospects joining us on this opportunity tele-seminar. Here is my up line talking about how they run their business and why it is beneficial for those that want to be called "*business builders*" to buy more product than necessary, because you could always give it away as samples.

That lasted three calls before I unplugged my team and new prospects from their opportunity/training calls and used only my own.

But I still had a problem: people and ego.

My up line was not too impressed to find out that I had unplugged my team from their training. I was accused of going rogue, not edifying them, being a lone soldier etc...

I told them that I hadn't changed anything from an edification perspective. I chose to lead my own organization as we all should eventually do anyway.

It was about that time that their ego kicked in.

You see, one of the things that I enjoy a lot is to train and speak in public. I would try and set up speaking engagements within and outside of the Direct Selling Profession. A lot of my speaking within the direct selling at that time was being passed down through this up line and they would recommend me.

Unfortunately, those engagements dried up because my up line decided not to support me anymore.

I wasn't allowed to speak from their stage anymore or be endorsed for my own speaking.

It was frustrating, but since then, all of my speaking engagements are a result of someone being in the audience or a direct referral from someone who was in the audience of a speech I made.

Unethical Practice #4 - Buying Your Way to the Top and Teaching Others to Do the Same.

This is a problem that exists to this day.

A spinoff from this buying your way to the top story happened in the spring of 2007.

The corporation created a special promotion for a home accessory product that would benefit everyone in the household, as well as offer the individual distributor the opportunity to generate some very good cash flow and commissions.

The corporation held a special event for certain leadership just prior to the launch of the promotion, and I was an attendee.

The corporation's idea was to offer this home accessory at 50% the normal cost to the distributor and leave the original point structure the same. Their intention was for the leadership to go back to our respective teams and market this promotion to our down line. The thought being, that if enough people purchased this home accessory for themselves (personal consumption), then everyone's organization and the corporation as a whole would get a big boost in volume sold.

I have never been accused of doing anything half assed. I looked at this opportunity and created a plan to really drive the volume in my own personal organization.

This home accessory retailed for a little over a thousand dollars and a distributor could purchase it at their cost which was a bit over $600.

So my idea was to bring back the good old days of direct selling.

What do I mean?

DIRECT SELLING!

The corporation's promotion was to leave the retail price at little over a thousand dollars and reduce the distributor cost to $350.

So, here is what I did.

First, I marketed this new promotion from the corporation directly to my organization, no strings attached. I explained the benefits and told them that they were not obligated, but should consider it if it fit their lifestyle.

The second thing I did was to contact the corporation to discuss if I could receive a "better" discount on the product if I bought them in bulk.

So, about a week later, I met with the corporation and made a deal to buy 500 units over a two month period. The stipulation that we agreed upon was that for each and every sale of one of these units, I would need to provide the corporation a copy of the purchase invoice with customer contact information, so that they could verify the sales.

Now I was in business, all I had to do was sell 500 units in two months and this little project of mine was going to generate a generous influx of cash. I would receive the difference between the retail price and my cost upfront and commissions for the volume on the back-end.

The real motivator was that if I could sell those 500 units within the two month period (July and August 2007) I would *"earn"* the next major level of compensation rank.

So with 60 days to go, I started to think about ways to sell these units. I couldn't advertise traditionally, so that was out. I could try and sell them door-to-door; I had a strong background in that method of sales.

Or, I could sell them in bulk! I implemented my own due diligence with regards to the new construction in my city (houses, apartments, condos etc...) and started contacting developers with my idea.

Within the first two weeks, I had commitments for all 500 units among seven different developers.

So, month number one finishes and my up line (who by the way I didn't tell that I was going to do this) start calling me from all over North America, because their volume all of a sudden took a significant leap upwards.

The next weekend, my up line from 4 levels above me and everyone in between decides to hold a training session in Toronto, so that I can "*train*" everyone on how to sell these home accessories.

This is a bad idea, a "*really*" bad idea.

Have you ever heard the most misused word or concept in direct selling: "*duplication?*"

Well, here I was back stage at this event with about 20 years of selling experience of which the last 2 years was consulting for a global tech giant to the Canadian banking industry.

My task was to take a concept that was based on selling experience, relationships and relationship building and teaching it to a room full of people that wouldn't have a clue as to how to approach a major developer.

I personally had a blast, since I love to train and I love to speak in public. Problem was this was really not a mass duplicable idea. Anyways, enough of that – let's get back to month number two of my 60 day sprint to the finish.

In the first week of the second month, I created the necessary paperwork and ensured that it was in the correct hands at corporate.

Customers were happy, I trained some of their trade's people on how to install them effectively and as a result, sold an additional 12 units and recruited 17 of these trades' people into my business.

About half way through the first week of the second month, I got a call from corporate about part of my up line trying to piggyback on my special pricing. The corporation was not very happy because of some rumors that started to float around about the way I sold these units. It is important to note that the corporation was happy with me and the deal because they received the paperwork that they requested and confirmed the sale of the units. As a matter of fact, they wouldn't ship them until they did confirm. I had asked them to stagger the distribution, so that 250 units were delivered and counted in July and then 250 units would be delivered and counted in August.

Let's get back to these rumors. One of my up lines decided to take the initiative after my training to recruit a few of his down line to try and attempt something similar to what I had achieved. The idea being, if one could do it, anyone could do it.

When I heard about these rumors it turned out to be this particular up line that was trashing me with my complete line of sponsorship.

It really got ugly, my LOS (Line of Sponsorship) was accepting these rumors at face value and they began questioning me about my sales, but mostly they were questioning my integrity.

I just kept on referring them to the corporation. If the customers are happy, which they were, and the corporation is happy, which they were because they confirmed each sale, then what's the problem? Thank God for paperwork!

Now if the above part wasn't bad enough, the next part will blow you mind.

Remember my up line that started all those rumors? Well guess what? He purchased about 200 units and made his "*dream team*" pay for them personally. These were kids. A few of them were under twenty, but it didn't seem to matter to him.

To say that it got ugly would be a significant understatement.

With 7 days to go before the end of the month, the last of the 250 units were delivered and counted, as well as fully backed up with paperwork.

I received a call from the Canadian corporate president who invited me to the head office for an informal ceremony. He wanted to congratulate me on my achievement but also to thank me for putting selling back into direct selling in the corporation.

That evening at an opportunity meeting I was to receive recognition for my achievement but instead, I was asked to leave the room and to meet with four levels of my line of sponsorship.

During that conversation I was accused of cheating and de-edifying my up line. Not one of them believed how I accomplished my sales. As a matter of fact, one particular senior up line member actually stated that there was no room for "*selling*" in "*his*" organization and if I would still like to be part of "*his*" team I best take my medicine.

My "*medicine*" was for them not to recognize me at the opportunity meeting or any major event in the near future.

A man with 35 years of experience in direct selling actually said to me that there was no room for selling in direct selling! Wow, it does take all kinds.

Five months later, I made an agreement with the corporation to resign from actively building my business without impact to my rank and status.

To this day, I still support my down line.

Unethical Practice #5 - It Takes All Kinds, Especially the Ones with Egos

There have been many more examples that I could have shared, but my goal was to help open your eyes to the challenges we have within our profession.

PART 2 - NEED FOR DISTRIBUTOR REPRESENTATION IN OUR PROFESSION

At the end of 2011 the estimated global population was slightly over 7 billion people. In the same year, the Direct Selling Profession exceeded 91.5 million people. This means that approximately 1 in 80 people on this planet are part of the Direct Selling Profession.

With $157 billion U.S. in retail sales being generated by these "non-represented" distributors, perhaps it's time that they get some much needed support. [ii]

The Direct Selling Member companies are well supported and lobbied for by their respective associations (WFDSA, DSA, etc.). However, what is seriously missing is an association that fully represents the individual distributor and offers them a voice.

This has been attempted in the past and has failed or fallen way short for one reason or another, however, it does not eliminate the need to have a voice dedicated to the individual distributor.

PART 3 - THE STAGGERING AMOUNT OF MISREPRESENTATION IN MLM/NETWORK MARKETING

As I have mentioned before, I am very proud of being a member of the Direct Selling Profession, however, what I am not proud of is having MLM/Network Marketing being described as *"...the direct descendent of classic, no-product pyramid schemes. With expansive pay plans and an endless chain of recruitment, MLM assumes both infinite and virgin markets – neither of which exists. MLM is therefore inherently flawed, uneconomic and deceptive."*

"To be successful in MLM, one must not only work hard, but one must also:

1.   *Be deceived*

2.   *Maintain a high level of self-deception*

3.   *Go about deceiving others*

4.   *Maintain denial of the harm done to those recruited into the chain or pyramid of participants.*

The degree of deception (and even total amounts in aggregate damages by MLMs as a group) exceeds the deceptions reported in the Bernie Madoff scandal and in the Enron stock scandal (plus WorldCom and Global Crossing). However, in the case of MLM, participants engage in self-deception as much as in deliberate misrepresentations. In short, the typical MLM is a composite lie, dependent on an endless chain of recruitment into a pyramid of participants who unwittingly engage in

17

massive theft by deception."iii

That's right, this sits on the Federal Trade Commission's website and I found it when I simply searched Google for *"list of direct selling companies investigated by FTC."*

PART 4 - MLM COMPANY COMMUNICATIONS AND THEIR MISREPRESENTATIONS AS "INCOME OPPORTUNITIES" OR "BUSINESS OPPORTUNITIES"

Often referred to as a *"distributor-only"* problem, this report offers statements that were direct quotes from MLM company web sites or promotional literature.

Companies cited in this report include: *"Advocare, Ameriplan, Amway (was "Quixtar" in the USA from 1999 to 2009), Arbonne Int'l, Cyberwize, Ecoquest (now Vollara), Fortune HiTech Marketing (FHTM), FreeLife International, Herbalife, Ignite -Stream Energy, Immunotec, iNetGlobal, Isagenix, Mannatech, Melaleuca, Mona Vie, MXI Corp. (Xocai), Nikken, Nu Skin, Reliv, SendOutCards, Sunrider, Symmetry, Tahitian Noni International, Tupperware, USANA, World Ventures , XANGO, Yor Health, Your Travel Biz (YTB)."*

The following are *"...ten categories of the typical misrepresentations (including those related to income) used to lure new recruits into joining and continuing to invest in an MLM - and to dupe regulators into accepting their abuses.*

- *Misrepresentations regarding MLM as a business model – compared to legitimate direct selling, pyramid schemes, etc...*

- *Misrepresentations comparing MLM to the job market, or to the stock market and other investments – even gambling*

- *Misrepresentations regarding legality, regulation, and legitimacy of MLM*

- *Misrepresentations regarding MLM products & services – product claims, prices, purchase quotas, stockpiling, investments in products and "tools for success," etc...*

- *Misrepresentations regarding MLM as a "business opportunity" and the importance of timing to take full advantage of it*

- *Misrepresentations regarding emphasis on recruitment over selling to non-participants – and on the recruitment process itself*

- *Misrepresentations regarding MLM compensation plans and promised or actual income from MLM participation*

- *Misrepresentations regarding success and failure, or retention and attrition (dropout) rates among MLM participants*

- *Misrepresentations about the personal benefits of MLM – time freedom, improved lifestyle, supportive associates, opportunity to help others, etc...*

- *Misrepresentations relating to credibility of the MLM, its leaders, and important persons whose names are somehow associated with it."* [iv]

The above four sections, as well as, examples are but a small example of unethical behavior in the Direct Selling Profession. The remainder of the book outlines my proposed solutions for this unethical behavior that continues to put a black mark on the direct selling profession.

CHAPTER 4
RAIDERS OF THE "LOST" DIRECT SELLER

In October 2009, I was invited to speak at a leadership retreat on the topic that I dubbed, *"Raiders of the 'Lost' Direct Seller."*

This talk was about the overwhelming examples of direct selling leaders who have implemented a strategy to grow their businesses that included raiding other companies' independent distributors, as well as, poaching independent distributors from within their own company.

Let us take a look at what the Direct Selling Association (DSA) has to say about raiding and poaching (called Proselyting).

"Proselyting is the term used to describe the art in direct selling of attempting to convert one or more sales force members from one company to another. The ethics and legality of efforts to attract salespeople from one company to another is a subject of frequent and intense discussion by industry members. The Direct Selling Association has adopted guidelines regarding these practices of which salespeople and companies should be aware. The guidelines and open letter set out below attempt to describe what the Association believes is the state of the law regarding such practices as well as acceptable direct selling business practice in this regard." [v]

AN OPEN LETTER TO DIRECT SELLERS FROM DSA PRESIDENT JOSEPH MARIANO

Occasionally, direct sellers in the field will be approached by other companies or their sales leaders with solicitations to join those companies. Sometimes, these solicitors present misinformation and denigrate the company you are with. Those solicitations can be inappropriate, unethical, misrepresentative, or even illegal and may be at odds with the Proselyting Guidelines of the Direct Selling Association (DSA). Under those guidelines, it is considered unethical behavior throughout the industry for one company to target the sales force of another company in an attempt to lure salespeople into their own organization and stop selling for their original company.

It is unfortunate when such behavior reflects poorly upon the direct selling industry and results in misinformation about our business being spread throughout our sales forces and the public. That is why we urge current direct sellers, or anyone who might be interested in a direct selling opportunity, to evaluate those opportunities on the basis of facts about the company doing the recruiting. Rumor or innuendo about other opportunities often prove to be just plain wrong. So when you're recruited, examine the appeal of the products offered, the attractiveness of the earning potential, and a company's commitment to the ideals and obligations embodied in the DSA Code of Ethics. Those are the factors most important to you in evaluating your current company or any future opportunity you may pursue.

All members of DSA are bound by our Code of Ethics and should follow our Proselyting Guidelines, which constitute our industry's ethical standard. To review our Code, please visit our website at www.dsa.org. We wish you strength, success, and growth in your direct selling career.

Sincerely,

Joseph N. Mariano

President

PROSELYTING GUIDELINES OF THE DIRECT SELLING ASSOCIATION

It is considered to be an improper practice when Company A, or its representatives, specifically and consciously target the sales force of Company B with the intent of persuading Company B's salespersons or employees not only to sell or work for Company A, but also to cease selling or working for Company B, thereby interfering with Company B's business or contractual relations. This is not intended to encompass the occasional incident or two, but it does apply to situations involving more than several persons, where the pattern, approach and timing of Company A would clearly indicate an intention to adversely impact on Company B. If Company B sends correspondence to Company A regarding alleged proselyting activity, Company A is expected to appropriately respond within 30 days after receipt of the correspondence.

FREQUENTLY ASKED QUESTIONS

What is proselyting?

When used in direct selling, proselyting simply describes the activity of a distributor for one direct selling company recruiting a distributor from another direct selling company. This may involve the recruiting distributor encouraging the other distributor to leave their current company or not. This could be a single isolated event or it could include an orchestrated effort by an individual recruiting distributor, group of distributors or the company to recruit many distributors from a particular company.

What are the DSA Proselyting Guidelines?

The DSA Proselyting Guidelines are aspirational in nature and declare what is considered an improper business practice with regards to proselyting.

Is the Proselyting Guidelines part of the DSA Code of Ethics?

No, the Proselyting Guidelines are not part of the DSA Code of Ethics and therefore are not enforced by the DSA Code Administrator.

Is proselyting restricted or prohibited by the DSA Code of Ethics or Proselyting Guidelines?

No, in general proselyting is not restricted or prohibited by the DSA Code of Ethics or Proselyting Guidelines. Proselyting is not covered by the DSA Code of Ethics. The Proselyting Guidelines simply declare specifically and consciously targeting another company's sales force with the intent to have them cease selling for their current company to be an improper business practice. The Proselyting Guidelines state:

"It is considered to be an improper business practice when Company A, or its representatives, specifically and consciously target the sales force of Company B with the intent of persuading Company B's salespersons or employees not only to sell or work for Company A, but also to cease selling or working for Company B, thereby interfering with Company B's business or contractual relations. This is not intended to encompass the occasional incident or two, but it does apply to situations involving more than several persons, where the pattern, approach and timing of Company A would clearly indicate an intention to adversely impact on

Company B.

If Company B sends correspondence to Company A regarding alleged proselyting activity, Company A is expected to appropriately respond within 30 days after receipt of the correspondence."

Is proselyting illegal in the United States?

No, in the United States proselyting is not illegal. However making a false or deceptive statement about a company or its products or services is a violation of law and the DSA Code of Ethics. Attempting to persuade a distributor to leave their current company could potentially be tortuous interference with a contract. The distributor that leaves a company may have legal restrictions placed on their activities under the contract they signed. They may, for instance, be prohibited from recruiting others from the sales force of the company they departed. They may be restricted from selling similar product lines for some reasonable period of time.

Why can't the DSA prohibit member companies from proselyting?

It is the view of the DSA Legal Department and DSA General Counsel that a blanket prohibition by DSA on proselyting would be violative of the law. Individuals, generally, are free to communicate with others and choose for whom they would like to work.

What can a company do if it thinks it is being targeted for proselyting?

Review and familiarizing yourself with the Proselyting Information Kit.

Gather as much objective information about the alleged activity as possible. This can included written statements from your sales force, letters, emails or other information that will substantiate the claim of proselyting. Rumors, hearsay and third-hand information is seldom accurate.

Contact the company that you have reason to believe is proselyting your sales force directly. It could be just a misunderstanding. They may not be aware of the activity. They may want to conduct their own internal investigation to determine the facts for themselves. They may be more than willing to resolve the complaint to your satisfaction. DSA is available to facilitate these communications, if desired.

If the matter cannot be resolved with step three, then you may seek mediation as outlined in the Proselyting Information kit. DSA is available to facilitate this as well.

The last resort is litigation, which can be costly, time consuming and still may not give you the result that you seek.[vi]

Back in October 2009 at my speech to the DSWA, I was unaware that one month prior, the then Executive Vice President & Legal Counsel for the Direct Selling Association, Joseph Mariano sent an internal memo to the Ethics and Self - Regulation Committee entitled, Proselyting and Direct Selling – A possible Action Plan and Recommendations.

As part of the background offered by Mr. Mariano to the Ethics committee was the following:

"The recently adopted World Federation of Direct Selling Associations (WFDSA) Model Code of Conduct, for example, suggests that constituent associations of WFDSA adopt Code of Ethics provisions which would prohibit the systematic enticement of sales force members from one company to another. However, U.S. antitrust considerations do not allow the USDSA to include such a provision in its Code. (See attached memorandum from Hogan & Hartson regarding proselyting and related association and industry antitrust and other legal issues.) Nonetheless, the suggested standard adopted by the WFDSA has given rise to the consideration by the Committee of ways in which DSA and its members, within the boundaries of U.S. law, might address certain proselyting disputes between companies.

This memo outlines ways in which DSA currently addresses the issue as well as several new initiatives for the Committee's consideration. All expansions of existing activities, as well as possible new programs, are suggested with the proviso that they need be implemented in a manner that will not result in a restraint of trade or otherwise restrict lawful competition among members."

POSSIBLE NEW DSA POLICIES

Several new and complementary alternative approaches might be considered by the Committee for implementation by the Association. Those options are outlined below.

Proselyting Education – DSA has several resources currently available regarding proselyting issues that might be better communicated and packaged, to be made available to various audiences.

Proselyting Information Kit –To include DSA's Guideline, Code Provisions, Open Letter, and Legal Memorandum

Ethics Seminar Programming – DSA's regular seminars, including the Annual meeting, DS 101, Ethics and Legal meetings could have "mandatory" sessions on proselyting legal and ethics considerations

Sales force Education – DSA could incorporate proselyting information in our frequent presentations to member company sales force members using the information described above tailored for those audiences

Ethics Recognition – DSA's existing ethics recognition program for member companies could be expanded to include a component regarding proselyting

DSEF Ethics Video Series – This existing and engaging web based video series could be expanded to include an appropriate module on proselyting and other sales force disputes

Direct Selling 411 – DSA's public/sales force oriented website, a growing resource for direct sellers, could include training materials on proselyting and a regular blog posting on the subject.[vii]

From my unique perspective the global direct selling community has gone as far as they can from a regulatory perspective. It is now up to us as leaders to take it forward.

One of the areas that I believe we can address is celebrating within the industry for what I would call "*abnormal*" growth.

Here is an example:

Direct selling leader A represents XYZ direct selling company. Then direct selling leader A chooses or is incentivized to move over to direct selling company ABC. Thirty days later, direct selling leader A at ABC company has "recruited" 1000+ distributors into his/her business.

Problem

The problem is two-fold and includes unethical practices by both a direct selling company and a direct selling leader. Let's examine them both.

Direct Selling Company ABC

The direct selling company has actively recruited an independent distributor (leader) with a proven track record to join their business. They also compensated that same independent distributor (leader) for making that move.

I cannot speak to the legality of these actions; however, these actions are truly unethical.

Direct Selling Independent Distributor (Leader)

This independent distributor (leader) chooses to move from direct selling company XYZ to ABC. That in itself is not unethical; however, I would state that the accepting of the incentivized compensation would constitute an unethical practice.

Let us look at the example once again and we see that this independent distributor (leader) has recruited 1000+ into his/her organization.

Where did all these "*new*" distributors come from? They are definitely not brand new direct selling independent distributors.

Without question the majority, if not all were "*proselytized.*"

What about the impact to these recruited distributors, not to mention the credibility of the profession?

As a profession, we need to raise our standards.

None of us wants to be "*regulated*" more, but is self-regulation really working?

I do not believe so.

This is a topic that I believe this book can help to address.

CHAPTER 5
HELP, I CAN'T FIND MY ETHICS!

How would you describe the condition of ethics in the world today? In the event that you happen to be like the majority of people, you are probably ashamed and therefore are sick and tired of men and women telling lies and men and women being unethical.

Lying and unethical practices spread throughout every facet of our lives. Let's take a look.

Traditional businesses: - Enron, Arthur Anderson, WorldCom, Adelphia Communications, Wal-Mart, Trafigura, DynCorp, Monsanto, Chevron, Blackwater, Dow Chemical, Union Carbide, Siemens, IBM, Halliburton, Raytheon, to identify but just a few examples.

Needless to say, the ethical problems we are witnessing aren't restricted to just the business world.

Education System - Don't need to look any farther than the Atlanta Public School System for an example.

Religions – Let us take at the recent allegations of child molestation, embezzlement, or worse in the Catholic Church.

Politicians - Let us just make it easy and say the majority of the Republican and Democratic parties.

Financial System - How about Goldman-Sachs, JP Morgan, the United States Senate, the United States House of Representatives.

I believe that it is fair to say that one particular reason the global stock markets keep going up and down like a yo-yo every single day is probably because investors simply do not know who to trust.

Criminal Justice System - How about misconduct and corruption in law enforcement, lawyers and judges.

Sports - Lance Armstrong, Tiger Woods, and Barry Bonds to name a few.

THE DIRECT SELLING PROFESSION IS NOT
EXEMPT FROM THIS "LIST OF SHAME"

Sadly, each and every day, somewhere around the world, an unethical business practice happens within the Direct Selling Profession.

Sure, several direct selling companies have been accused of unethical behaviour such as: "Advocare, Ameriplan, Amway (was "Quixtar" in the USA from 1999 to 2009), Arbonne Int'l, Cyberwize, Ecoquest (now Vollara), Fortune HiTech Marketing (FHTM), FreeLife International, Herbalife, Ignite -Stream Energy, Immunotec, iNetGlobal, Isagenix, Mannatech, Melaleuca, Mona Vie, MXI Corp. (Xocai), Nikken, Nu Skin, Reliv, SendOutCards, Sunrider, Symmetry, Tahitian Noni International, Tupperware, USANA, World Ventures , XANGO, Yor Health, Your Travel Biz (YTB)." [viii]

It should not come as a surprise to you to find out that the large majority of these companies have had their ethics questioned. However, bear in mind one key element, a direct selling company is merely an entity comprised of a bunch of direct sellers. And therein lays the problem.

"The best thing about being part of the Direct Selling Profession is the people. The worst part about being part of the Direct Selling Profession is the people." - Kevin McNabb

Do We Have an Ethical Dilemma Within the Direct Selling Profession?

Numerous discussions about ethics and unethical practices are generally established based on arguments about the suitable definition. Ethics is unique among professions in that experts frequently are unable to agree on a standard definition of an ethical dilemma. Therefore, for the purpose of this book, I am going to utilize the following definition of *"ethical dilemma."*

"This is an ethical problem in which the ethical choice involves ignoring a powerful non-ethical consideration. Do the right thing, but lose your job, a friend, a lover, or an opportunity for advancement. A non-ethical consideration can be powerful and important enough to justify choosing it over the strict ethical action." [ix]

Exactly why have ethics over the last few decades in the Direct Selling Profession been in such a bad condition?

Allow us to have a look at a number of the reasons why a direct selling distributor would make unethical choices.

When a direct seller makes unethical choices, they do so for one of three reasons:

Regrettably the Average Direct Selling Professional Truly Does What's Most Hassle-free

As Direct Selling Professionals, we appear to continuously fail individual ethics tests.

As Direct Selling Professionals, we will do things despite the fact that we understand that they're inappropriate.

As Direct Selling Professionals, we will do these inappropriate things, perhaps because we believe that we won't get caught.

As Direct Selling Professionals, we use the justification of being stressed to cut corners and we justify that it's going to happen just one more time. Is this the ethical way of dealing with stress?

Direct Selling Professionals Will Do Whatever They Believe They Must Do To Obtain a Victory

Most Direct Selling Professionals detest losing.

Most successful Direct Selling Professionals that I know desire to win through personal and organizational achievement. However, the downside is that many believe they need to choose between being ethical and being successful.

Many Direct Selling Professionals believe that embracing ethics would limit their choices, their opportunities, and their ability to succeed in the world of direct selling. It's the old suspicion that good guys finish last.

If Direct Selling Professionals believes that they have just two choices, to win by doing whatever it takes, even if it's unethical or to have ethics and lose, they are faced with a real moral dilemma. Few Direct Selling Professionals set out with the desire to be dishonest, but no one wants to lose.

A Direct Selling Professional Will certainly Justify Their Options With Relativism

Many Direct Selling Professionals decide to cope with such no-win scenarios simply by choosing what's appropriate in the moment, based on their circumstances. Their own perception that principles such as right and wrong, goodness and badness, or truth and falsehood are not absolute however, varies from culture to culture and situation to situation.

Dr. Joseph Fletcher - The Founder of the Situational Ethics Movement

Joseph Fletcher, an Anglican theologian, developed situation ethics in the 1960s after critiquing legalism and antinomianism. Legalism is the belief that there are fixed moral laws that must always be obeyed. Antinomianism is the belief that there are no fixed moral principles and that ethics should be spontaneous.

Fletcher believed that neither legalism nor antinomianism provided a sound basis for ethics and advocated "*situationism*" as a compromise. His book, Situation Ethics, was the centerpiece of his critique and founded much of the modern situation ethics movement.

According to Fletcher, decision-making should be based on the circumstances of a particular situation, and not on fixed law. He believed that truth is relative and that love is the only absolute. Thus, he believed that as long as love is the intention, the end justifies the means.

Ironically, Fletcher claims he founded his model on a biblical statement found in 1 John 4:8: "God is love." Yet he apparently didn't realize that the same book says commandment keeping shows our love for God (1 John 5:3) and that God never approves of law breaking. Indeed, such conduct is sinful (1 John 3:4). [x]

What eventually happened to Fletcher? His conclusion that God's Word wasn't enough to guide decision-making led him to become an avid supporter of euthanasia and abortion. He died in 1991 an atheist.

The profession of direct selling unfortunately has not been spared the spread of "*situational ethics.*"

The outcome is ethical turmoil. Each and every direct seller has his/her own ethical standards, which usually transform from situation to situation.

It is fascinating to note that even though our decisions at one time were based on ethics, now ethics are based on our decisions. If it's good for me, then it's good. Where is this trend likely to end?

Let's take a look at what would happen if we applied this trend to direct selling:

What Would Happen If A Direct Selling Professional Always Did What Was Most Convenient?

What if all of us decided, as direct sellers, to just manage each and every situation based on what was most convenient to us? Not over a short period of time, but over a long period of time. What do you think would happen to our relationships with our down-line? What about our relationships with our up-line? How about our relationships with our customers? Answer: **Total disaster.**

What Would Happen If a Direct Selling Professional believed that they have to do whatever is Necessary to Seek Victory?

As Direct Selling Professionals, our entire businesses rely on the relationships we have with the direct selling distributors who are part of our organization. As inter-dependent business owners, if we tried to "*win*" each and every transaction or interaction with our down line distributors, over time those relationships will die off. The best way to make sure that both your business and your relationships with your down line distributors grow is to seek out a win-win scenario for each transaction and/or interaction.

What If A Direct Selling Professional Decided To Handle A No-Win Situation By Deciding What Was Right In The Moment, Or According To Their Circumstances?

As a Direct Selling Professional, or even as a human being for that matter, waiting until the last moment to decide how to handle a situation without a proper moral compass will end in disaster sooner rather than later.

There needs to be a better way. There is.

WHAT'S THAT? IS THE GLOBAL MARKETPLACE ALTERING ITS BEHAVIOR?

I am aware that from time to time it may not appear this way; however there appears to be an ever-increasing desire for ethical practices in business, and as far as I can see, this desire reaches the very summit of the Direct Selling Profession.

With regards to business, the entire world is shrinking; the international marketplace is increasingly more accessible with each day and every transaction. Despite the fact that business has brought people closer together, culture and traditions will always be in some sort of conflict.

Whenever you are working in business with people of other cultures, it is very important to understand the differences. It's vital that you recognize that the international marketplace is a diverse marketplace, and that your potential customers may possess different perspectives on ethics and appropriate behavior than those with which you are familiar.

As Direct Selling Professionals, we are the CEOs of our own corporations, and even though these corporations are managed from our homes, they are multimillion-dollar opportunities and thus should reflect the highest ethical standards expected on the global stage.

It's exciting to realize that there is a desire to have change with respect to ethics in our culture. The sad news is that most Direct Selling Professionals don't seem to understand how to make that transition.

Keep in mind that the moment you step into the global marketplace, you really need to be in a global frame of mind. Bid farewell to conventional American jargon and opt for common, direct and courteous ways of communicating your thoughts, beliefs and ideas.

Furthermore, take the time to research the country and the culture of those with whom you will be interacting. It is important that you know the boundaries when it comes to asking personal questions. What you think is polite chitchat could actually be an offensive question to someone else.

Getting into the global marketplace is a challenging, but extremely rewarding, endeavor if you do it right. Just be sure that you're informed and ready to take on the responsibilities involved, and you'll find the global marketplace is a great place for your business to be.

WHY THE DIRECT SELLING PROFESSION SHOULD NOT FOLLOW THE TREND OF THE GLOBAL MARKETPLACE

So why shouldn't the Direct Selling Profession follow the trend of the global marketplace where it pertains to ethics?

Take a look at how the global marketplace is currently trying to address the problem of ethics in business. They are:

Asking other individuals to take on the responsibility of instructing our organizations about ethics.

Some companies have outsourced the task of training ethics to their employees, so that in the event of wrongdoing, the company can attempt to evade punishment for failure to comply with governmental guidelines.

Turning a blind eye to the problem, or insufficiently reprimanding the individual for unacceptable behavior.

Instead of a company taking a proactive approach to teach their employees proper ethical standards, some global companies have decided to deal with the ethical offenders only when caught.

This seems a lot like closing the barn doors after the horses have escaped.

Depending on the laws of the municipality, state, or country to address the problem.

Here is the saddest of them all. Some companies have actually given up entirely on deciding what's ethical and instead are using what's legal as their standard for decision-making. Any wonder why we have the problem we do in the global marketplace?

Let's apply these "*solutions*" to the Direct Selling Profession. How do you think these solutions would be received within our global community?

Would you really want to hand over to an "*unknown*" source how your business should be run and how your down-line should be treated? I hope your answer is no. If you're unsure of this answer, you may want to think about a career change.

How about waiting until someone gets caught, even though you know that they're doing something wrong. Is that the way you would want your business to be run, or to have your down-line run their business?

Once again, I hope your answer is no.

Would you like to rely on the law to manage your business? Since most direct selling businesses represent global opportunities, relying on the law becomes next to impossible, if not reprehensible.

What do I mean by that? The last place a direct selling professional or the profession of direct selling, wants to leave their destiny is in the hands of any government.

The profession of direct selling is truly the last bastion of free enterprise. It has broken down more walls and opened up more freedom opportunities to direct sellers on this globe than any other single business-related idea to hit this planet. I implore you to fully understand the area of free enterprise, and once you do, you'll fully understand the power of direct selling.

Also known as a "free market", which is an economic system in which people are allowed to choose their own jobs, start private businesses, and make a profit in any legal way that is controlled very little by the government.

WE SHOULD TAKE THIS PERSONALLY AS DIRECT SELLING PROFESSIONALS

In today's modern society we have arrived at the belief that ethics is either a business issue or a political issue. In actuality it is neither, it is a personal issue.

As Direct Selling Professionals we say we would like integrity. However at the same time, ironically, a large amount of Direct Selling Professionals don't always act with the kind of integrity they expect from others.

As an example, the same Direct Selling Professional who cheats on his taxes or steals office supplies, demands honesty and integrity from the corporation whose stock he buys, the politician he votes for, and the customer he deals with in his own business.

It's an easy task to talk about ethics and even easier to be embarrassed with Direct Selling Professionals who fall short in the ethics evaluation, particularly when we have been violated by the wrongdoing of other Direct Selling Professionals. It's more difficult to make ethical choices in our own lives. When we as Direct Selling Professionals are faced with objectionable alternatives, what are we going to do?

ETHICS AND THE FINAL WORD

I recognize the need to constantly strive to be ethical, and it is my personal belief that you do as well. I am also a firm believer that it must be possible to do what's right 100% of the time and still be successful in business.

Paradigm: Direct Selling Professionals who are committed to carrying out what's right and also have a personal dedication to social responsibility, and who consistently act on it, will be more profitable in the long-run than those who don't.

Now I am not implying that if you embrace ethical behavior you will automatically be rich and successful. That would be foolish. However, it will create a solid foundation on which to build a successful business.

Let's discuss returning to fundamentals. Just how are you aware of what's right? Precisely how do you find the way through perhaps the most challenging of stress-filled situations?

Exactly where can you locate a standard that will work in every situation, a guide that will assist you to sleep nicely at night, succeed as a Direct Selling Professional, transform your relationships, and have confidence that you're doing all you can every time?

Answer: Read on.

OBSERVATIONS FROM
THE RESPONSIBLE DIRECT SELLER™

All of us as Direct Selling Professionals possess a great ethical obligation to try and do what's right at all times. One particular element, however, is definitely standing in our way: we are human beings!

Regrettably, for as long as there are men and women involved with business, we are going to continue to have questionable ethics in the Direct Selling Profession. That is, unless "*we*" as individual men and women, as well as a profession, make a decision to change.

Most Direct Selling Professionals desire to change their business, local community, or family situation without having to change themselves. News Flash: It does not work that way.

We have to stop spending time attempting to change others and begin focusing all of our time on changing ourselves. If enough Direct Selling Professionals did that, the impact would be exponential.

Are there ethically questionable direct selling companies? Oh, probably. However, the real challenge is that some direct selling companies have some ethically questionable Direct Selling Professionals associated with their company as distributors.

How can we change as individuals and ensure that "*we*" are not part of the problem, but part of the solution?

To start, under no circumstances do anything because it is convenient, where it pertains to building your business. Always do what is "right," even if it impacts you financially. Do not think short-term; always have a big picture attitude.

Look for real win-win scenarios in all your interactions. Make sure that with this strategy, the other person wins first. This will go a long way to building stronger relationships.

Make decisions ahead of time on how you will handle situations within your business. This way, you will not be forced to continually make decisions on the fly that will lead to unethical behavior.

Do not worry what other direct sellers are doing in the marketplace. Only worry about what you are doing. Clean up your own backyard, before even thinking about pointing to someone else's.

Be responsible for your business. Do not rely on others to determine what is right and wrong. If you see something wrong in your business (this includes your down-line), make the correction and move on. Waiting until it corrects itself is a recipe for disaster.

There is a solution to every problem. You just have to take a moment and look for it. Be part of the solution, not the problem.

CHAPTER 6
HOW ABOUT AN ETHICAL "GOLD STANDARD"?

Precisely how would you as a Direct Selling Professional rate yourself with regards to integrity and ethics? In our profession, many statistics are measured, such as, lead generation, recruiting, volume, and in some cases personal growth. Rarely does one measure their level of integrity and ethics. But what if you did? What if you knew where you stood today from an ethical perspective, as well as, where you would like to be? Would this be beneficial to you and your organization? Of course it would, let's take a look at ourselves for a moment.

It all starts at home. Far too often we are concerned about what others think of us, or how they would react to what we are thinking. This being the case, I highly recommend that we all start by cleaning up our own ethical backyard first. Then we don't have to worry about what others think about us, because we will know that we are on a strong ethical path.

For the purpose of this discussion, allow us to sort Direct Selling Professionals into one of the five general categories below:

- As a Direct Selling Professional, I am at all times ethical.

- As a Direct Selling Professional, I am primarily ethical.

- As a Direct Selling Professional, I am to some degree ethical.

- As a Direct Selling Professional, I am infrequently ethical.

- As a Direct Selling Professional, I am never ever ethical.

So, which one of the statements above is applicable to you? Precisely how would you define yourself? How would others define you? Now I am not asking what statement you would like to best describe you, however, that would be important to know from a growth perspective. Be honest with yourself and place a checkmark next to the statement that is most applicable to you. (It's OK, no one is looking!)

THE KEY REASONS WHY ETHICS SHOULD MAKE A DIFFERENCE TO A DIRECT SELLING PROFESSIONAL

Now, hopefully you have been honest with yourself and placed a checkmark next to one of the statements above that best describes you. Let us now take a look at how men and women in our profession view ethics.

The vast majority of Direct Selling Professionals place themselves within the first or second category (at all times ethical or primarily ethical). The majority of men and women attempt to be ethical much of the time.

Virtually all Direct Selling Professionals who consider themselves to be "*primarily ethical*," do so as a result of individual opportuneness. Discord is undesirable. Exercising self-discipline is undesirable. Being defeated is unfavorable. A wide variety of Direct Selling Professionals who consider themselves to be "primarily ethical," choose this direction simply because they don't wish to cope with those distractions.

Virtually all Direct Selling Professionals feel that staying "*primarily ethical*" is okay, except in cases where these men and women happen to be on the losing end of another individual's breach in ethics.

One particular guideline can assist Direct Selling Professionals to transfer from "*primarily ethical*" to "*at all time's ethical*" and shut the gap between the first two categories.

Imagine if you happen to be presented with a code of conduct (besides the codes of conduct outlined by the World Federation of Direct Selling Associations or your local Direct Selling Association) or perhaps a moral compass to help you govern all your ethical decision-making, would you use it?

What if this moral compass was accessible to the masses and transcended all global cultures? Now would you use it?

Do you believe a global moral compass really exists? I truly believe that one does: It exists perfectly in what we have coined the "*Golden Rule*."

Idiom: "*do unto others as you would have them do unto you*"

What would our profession be like if all Direct Selling Professionals behaved toward others as they would like to have others behave toward them?

The Golden Rule is mentioned throughout just about every ancient writing about behavioral precepts (including the New Testament,

Talmud, Koran, and the Analects of Confucius). Among the earliest appearances in English is Earl Rivers' translation of a saying of Socrates (Dictes and Sayenges of the Philosophirs, 1477): *"Do to other as thou wouldst they should do to thee, and do to none other but as thou wouldst be done to."* It is so well known that it is often shortened.

By inquiring, *"How would I like to be treated in this situation?"* you have accessed one of the most powerful principles in the world.

As a Direct Selling Professional, are you considering disregarding my pronouncement? In the event that is the situation, then most likely you could possibly be ensnared in the entanglement of modern day thinking on ethics.

Permit me to demonstrate why the *"Golden Rule"* can be used as an ethical compass and why it will always point you in the right direction.

Individual Rules? How About One Guideline for Everyone?

An example of the Golden Rule is available in nearly each and every culture. In the chart below you will see a number of adaptations on the Golden Rule:

Religion	Description
Bahai	*"And if thine eyes be turned towards justice, choose thou for thy neighbor that which thou choosest for thyself."* [xi]
Buddhism	*"Hurt not others with that which pains yourself."*[xii]
Christianity	*"Whatever you want men to do to you, do also to them."*[xiii]
Confucianism	*"What you do not want done to yourself, do not do to others."* [xiv]
Commonsensism	*"Treat people the way you'd like to be treated."*[xv]
Hinduism	*"This is the sum of duty; do naught unto others what you would not have them do unto you."* [xvi]

Islam	*"No one of you is a believer until he loves for his neighbor what he loves for himself."* [xvii]
Jainism	*"A man should wander about treating all creatures as he himself would be treated."* [xviii]
Judaism	*"What is hateful to you, do not do to your fellow man. This is the entire law; all the rest is commentary."* [xix]
Yoruba Proverb (Nigeria)	"One going to take a pointed stick to pinch a baby bird should first try it on himself to feel how it hurts." [xx]
Zoroastrianism	"Whatever is disagreeable to yourself, do not do unto others." [xxi]

Based upon the examples above, it's really clear to me that the Golden Rule is available to virtually every culture and religion, as well as available to all Direct Selling Professionals no matter where they reside on the planet. Without question, the Golden Rule is actually the best example of a worldwide guideline for ethics as it is possible to find. Generally there are really only two significant factors when it comes to the subject of ethics:

1. A standard to follow.

2. The will to follow it.

Ethics is actually related to how we as Direct Selling Professionals satisfy the difficult task of carrying out the appropriate thing when that "*thing*" will impact us much more as compared to what we are prepared to pay. Truth is there are two elements to ethics: the first consists of the capability to be able to determine correct from incorrect, acceptable from depraved, and congruity from incongruity. The second entails the dedication to carry out what is appropriate, good as well as correct. Ethics requires us as Direct Selling Professionals to take action; it is definitely not just a subject to consider or dispute.

POWERFUL REASONS WHY YOU AND I AS DIRECT SELLING PROFESSIONALS SHOULD EMBRACE THIS GUIDELINE

Some of you may be thinking, *"Kevin, how can you be so naive?"* I recognize that not necessarily every person is searching for a straightforward, sensible, and relevant guideline to live their life ethically, OK. Unfortunately, some men and women in the Direct Selling Profession actually choose to lie, defraud, and steal, in addition to doing much worse. Other men and women just want to deliberate and dispute ideas. However, men and women in the Direct Selling Profession, who would like to discover an excellent, trustworthy custom of ethical behavior to live their lives by, can discover it in the Golden Rule. Here is exactly why I believe this in all my heart:

THIS ETHICAL COMPASS IS ACCEPTED BY THE MAJORITY OF DIRECT SELLING PROFESSIONALS

The likelihood is very good that you possess a strong familiarity with exactly how broadly recognized the Golden Rule has become. Nevertheless if you just aren't completely convinced, I believe that a powerful case can also be devised for the Golden Rule according to common sense.

Are you able to envision an individual saying, "Please whatever you do, treat me worse than I treat you, OK"? Absolutely not going to happen in your lifetime. Every man or woman in our profession desires to be dealt with in a respectful manner. Even men and women who engage in destructive relationships or who happen to participate in detrimental behaviour don't really wish or even purposefully seek out poor treatment from other men and women. It is really not illogical for any Direct Selling Professional to desire good treatment from other Direct. Neither is it asking far too much to expect men and women to treat other men and women properly.

It is extremely challenging for Direct Selling Professionals to rationalize the demanding of superior treatment from other Direct Selling Professionals than they are willing to offer. Exactly what could they base it on? How about income generation? In the event that's the situation, then the Direct Selling Professional generating $100,000 a month who wants superior treatment from someone making $25,000 per month will need to consent to being dealt with improperly by those who make $500,000 a month!

What if Direct Selling Professionals actually based treatment of others on expertise? Or what if Direct Selling Professionals based their treatment of others on political affiliation or personally held beliefs?

You can understand exactly where this could certainly end up. Regardless of what haphazard requirements you can imagine, no matter whether its income generation, expertise, ideology, nationality, race, or something else entirely, it simply cannot end up being rationally reinforced. This type of misguided application would ultimately become just like a giant game of king of the hill. Perhaps you have played that game as a child? One individual ascends upwards on top of a hill and attempts to remain there whilst everyone else attempts to topple them off the top. The only method to win the game is usually to be the biggest bully. And in many cases if you do win the game, you get rather pummeled along the way.

One of the primary principles in human relationships is to seek out mutual understanding with other men and women. That's an outstanding guideline regardless of whether you're discovering a brand new relationship, meeting with a prospective customer, coaching a member of your down line, uniting with your children, or experiencing a spirited discussion with your significant other. Comparing and contrasting related experiences and discovering shared beliefs can pave the way for successful relationships. The Golden Rule enables you to develop mutual understanding with any other man or women.

THIS ETHICAL COMPASS IS STRAIGHTFORWARD AS WELL AS SIMPLE TO COMPREHEND.

As Direct Selling Professionals we quite often experience difficulty comprehending the subject matter of ethics mainly because it appears to be complicated as well as intangible. One of many wonderful things about the Golden Rule would be that it helps make the abstract discernible. The application is simply not about comprehending the law. It is not a philosophical exercise. You merely visualize yourself in the place of the other person. Even a tiny child can understand that simple concept. There aren't any complex protocols and absolutely no escape clauses.

Now it is extremely important to say at this stage that not each and every ethical situation can be resolved instantaneously by utilizing the Golden Rule. Sometimes the most challenging part of asking *"How would I like to be treated in this situation?"* is distinguishing who may very well be impacted by the specific situation and what impact it may have on them. However for even the most sophisticated challenges, if you take the time to give the subject some consideration, you are able to more often than not figure it out.

WITH THIS ETHICAL COMPASS EVERYONE WINS

Perhaps you have had the displeasure of meeting men and women in the Direct Selling Profession who actually believe that in order for them to be those who succeed, other men and women need to be made to lose? I know that I have, and in most cases you can see them coming from a mile away. These Direct Selling Professionals view absolutely everyone as a possible adversary who actually needs to be squashed, or these men and women take advantage of the discomfort of other men and women so that they can succeed.

Could you imagine if your direct selling company decided to implement a new compensation package that allowed you to financially benefit from destruction or weaknesses of your down line? Would you consider this to be ethical or morally reprehensible?

Not everyone believes that financial gain from morally reprehensible or socially irresponsible sectors of our society is a bad thing. Take for example a Mutual Fund investment offered by USAMutuals.com called the "Vice Fund." They believe that "Dividends and Cash Flow Do Matter," even if you are investing in such sectors as Aerospace/Defense, Gaming, Tobacco or Alcoholic Beverages. [xxii]

"The Vice Fund invests in companies, both domestic and foreign, engaged in the aerospace and defense industries, owners and operators, gaming facilities as well as manufacturers of gaming equipment, manufactures of tobacco products and producers of alcoholic beverages.

The Vice Fund seeks to select well-performing stocks of tobacco, alcohol, gaming, and weapons/defense companies because we believe that these industries tend to thrive regardless of the economy as a whole. In fact, they may have the potential to perform better when times are uncertain, leading many to view investment in "Vice" industries as a solid strategy during recessionary periods."

In a world where the focus always seems to be on one winner and one loser, perhaps the philosophy behind the Golden Rule will help ground us and offer a true win-win opportunity.

THIS ETHICAL COMPASS WILL ALWAYS POINT YOU IN THE RIGHT DIRECTION

The Golden Rule really does more than merely offer men and women victories. What's more, it possesses inner value for each and every Direct Selling Professional who actually chooses to exercise this option. Within a world involving significant ambiguity, I truly believe that numerous men and women in the Direct Selling Profession are searching for the proper path. The Golden Rule can supply that for you or anyone that you know. The Golden Rule under no circumstances ever changes. It provides sound, foreseeable direction each and every time it's utilized. And greatest thing of all, the Golden Rule actually works.

THE "GOLD STANDARD" FOR BEST PLACES TO WORK FOR

Sixteen years ago, Fortune Magazine started a list of the "100 Best Companies to Work For" that took into consideration more than just revenue and philanthropic endeavors.

This year in 2013, for the second year in a row, Google was ranked as being the #1 Best Companies to Work For. However precisely what makes Google so great to work for? The Internet marketing leader takes the 100 Best Companies to Work for crown for the fourth time, and not merely for the One hundred Thousand hours of sponsored massage therapy it allocated to employees during 2012. New in 2013 are three wellness centers and a seven-acre sports complex, which features a roller hockey rink; courts for basketball, bocce, and shuffle ball; and horseshoe pits. [xxiii]

THE GOOGLE CULTURE

It's actually the men and women that make Google the sort of company it is. Google hires men and women who are smart and determined, and they favor potential over experience. Although Googlers as they are called internally share common goals and visions for the company, they originate from all avenues of life and speak a multitude of languages, reflecting the global audience that they serve. And when away from work, Googlers pursue passions ranging from cycling to beekeeping, from

Frisbee to foxtrot.

They strive to preserve the open culture often associated with start-ups, in which everyone is a hands-on contributor and feels confident expressing ideas and opinions. In their weekly all-hands ("TGIF") meetings, not to mention over email or in the cafe, Googlers ask questions directly to Larry, Sergey and other execs about any number of company issues. Their workplaces and restaurants are created to inspire interactions between Googlers within and across teams, as well as to ignite discussion about business as well as play.

What Google Believes

10 things Google knows to be true - Google first wrote these "10 things" when they were just a few years old. Occasionally they take another look at this list to determine if it continues to hold true. Google hopes it does, and you are able to hold them to that.

1.   **Concentration on the End User and All Else Follows**. Since the very beginning, Google has concentrated on supplying the best user experience possible. Regardless of whether they're creating a new Internet browser or a new adjustment to the look of the homepage, Google takes great care to make certain that they're going to ultimately serve you, rather than their own internal goal or bottom line. Their homepage interface is clear and simple, and pages load instantly. Placement in search results is never sold to anyone, and advertising is not only clearly marked as such, it offers relevant content and is not distracting. And when they build new tools and applications, they believe they should work so well you don't have to consider how they might have been designed differently.

2.   **It's Far Better to Carry out One Thing Really, Really Well**. Google does search. With one of the world's largest research groups focused exclusively on solving search problems, Google knows what they do well, and how they could do it better. Through continued iteration on difficult problems, they've been able to solve complex issues and provide continuous improvements to a service that already makes finding information a fast and seamless experience for millions of people. Their dedication to improving search helps them apply what they've learned to new products, like Gmail and Google Maps. Their hope is to bring the power of search to previously unexplored areas, and to help people access and use even more of the ever-expanding information in their lives.

3.   **Fast Is Better Than Slow**. Google knows your time is valuable, so when you're seeking an answer on the web you want it right away, and they aim to please. Google may be the only people in the world who can say their goal is to have people leave their website as quickly as possible. By shaving excess bits and bytes from their pages and increasing the efficiency of their serving environment, they've broken their own speed records many times over, so that the average response time on a search result is a fraction of a second. Google keeps speed in mind with each new product they release, whether it's a mobile application or Google Chrome, a browser designed to be fast enough for the modern web. And they continue to work on making it all go even faster.

4.   **Democracy on the Web Works**. Google search works because it relies on the millions of individuals posting links on websites to help determine which other sites offer content of value. They assess the importance of every web page using more than 200 signals and a variety of techniques, including their patented PageRank™ algorithm, which analyzes which sites have been "voted" to be the best sources of information by other pages across the web. As the web gets bigger, this approach actually improves, as each new site is another point of information and another vote to be counted. In the same vein, they are active in open source software development, where innovation takes place through the collective effort of many programmers.

5.   **You Don't Need To Be At Your Desk To Need An Answer**. The world is increasingly mobile: people want access to information wherever they are, whenever they need it. They're pioneering new technologies and offering new solutions for mobile services that help people all over the globe to do any number of tasks on their phone, from checking email and calendar events to watching videos, not to mention the several different ways to access Google search on a phone. In addition, they're hoping to fuel greater innovation for mobile users everywhere with Android, a free, open source mobile platform. Android brings the openness that shaped the Internet to the mobile world. Not only does Android benefit consumers, who have more choice and innovative new mobile experiences, but it opens up revenue opportunities for carriers, manufacturers and developers.

6.   **You Can Make Money Without Doing Evil**. Google is a business. The revenue they generate is derived from offering search technology to companies and from the sale of advertising displayed on their site and on other sites across the web. Hundreds of thousands of

advertisers worldwide use Ad Words to promote their products; hundreds of thousands of publishers take advantage of their AdSense program to deliver ads relevant to their site content. To ensure that they're ultimately serving all their users (whether they are advertisers or not), Google has a set of guiding principles for their advertising programs and practices:

a.   They don't allow ads to be displayed on their results pages unless they are relevant where they are shown. And they firmly believe that ads can provide useful information if, and only if, they are relevant to what you wish to find - so it's possible that certain searches won't lead to any ads at all.

b.   They believe that advertising can be effective without being flashy. They don't accept pop-up advertising, which interferes with your ability to see the content you've requested. They've found that text ads that are relevant to the person reading them draw much higher click through rates than ads appearing randomly. Any advertiser, whether small or large, can take advantage of this highly targeted medium.

c.   Advertising on Google is always clearly identified as a *Sponsored Link*," so it does not compromise the integrity of their search results. They never manipulate rankings to put their partners higher in their search results and no one can buy better PageRank. Their users trust their objectivity and no short-term gain could ever justify breaching that trust.

7.   **There's Always More Information Out There**. Once they'd indexed more of the HTML pages on the Internet than any other search service, their engineers turned their attention to information that was not as readily accessible. Sometimes it was just a matter of integrating new databases into search, such as adding a phone number and address lookup and a business directory. Other efforts required a bit more creativity, like adding the ability to search news archives, patents, academic journals, billions of images and millions of books. And their researchers continue looking into ways to bring the entire world's information to people seeking answers.

8.   **The Need For Information Crosses All Borders**. Google was founded in California, but their mission is to facilitate access to information for the entire world, and in every language. To that end, they have offices in more than 60 countries, maintain more than 180 Internet

domains, and serve more than half of their results to people living outside the United States. They offer Google's search interface in more than 130 languages, offer people the ability to restrict results to content written in their own language, and aim to provide the rest of our applications and products in as many languages and accessible formats as possible. Using their translation tools, people can discover content written on the other side of the world in languages they don't speak. With these tools and the help of volunteer translators, they have been able to greatly improve both the variety and quality of services they can offer in even the most far-flung corners of the globe.

9. **You Can Be Serious Without A Suit**. Google founders built Google around the idea that work should be challenging, and the challenge should be fun. They believe that great, creative things are more likely to happen with the right company culture-and that doesn't just mean lava lamps and rubber balls. There is an emphasis on team achievements and pride in individual accomplishments that contribute to our overall success. They put great stock in their employees-energetic, passionate people from diverse backgrounds with creative approaches to work, play and life. Their atmosphere may be casual, but as new ideas emerge in a café line, at a team meeting or at the gym, they are traded, tested and put into practice with dizzying speed-and they may be the launch pad for a new project destined for worldwide use.

10. **Great Just Isn't Good Enough**. They see being great at something as a starting point, not an endpoint. They set themselves goals they know they can't reach yet, because they know that by stretching to meet them they can get further than they expected. Through innovation and iteration, they aim to take things that work well and improve upon them in unexpected ways. For example, when one of their engineers saw that search worked well for properly spelled words, he wondered about how it handled typos. That led him to create an intuitive and more helpful spell checker.

Even if you don't know exactly what you're looking for, finding an answer on the web is our problem, not yours. They try to anticipate needs not yet articulated by their global audience, and meet them with products and services that set new standards. When they launched Gmail, it had more storage space than any email service available. In retrospect offering that seems obvious, but that's because now they have new standards for email storage. Those are the kinds of changes they seek to make, and they're always looking for new places where they can make a difference. Ultimately, their constant dissatisfaction with the way things are becomes the driving force behind everything they do.

What Google Does For You

Larry Page, Google co-founder and CEO, once described the *"perfect search engine"* as something that "understands exactly what you mean and gives you back exactly what you want." Since he spoke those words Google has grown to offer products beyond search, but the spirit of what he said remains. With all their technologies, from search to Chrome to Gmail, their goal is to make it as easy as possible for you to find the information you need and get the things you need to do done.

This means making search smarter and faster, so it can understand that when you type [jaguar] you're looking for the car, not photos of the animal. It means showing you when your friends like an ad or a search result, so that you know it might be valuable. It means making their products work intuitively, so that you can share documents with Gmail contacts without having to copy and paste, and open the same tabs on your Android phone that you have open on your Chrome browser on your desktop. Above all, it means making their products work better so that people can spend time on the stuff they're good at, like enjoying time with family, camping in the wilderness, painting a picture or throwing a party. They're not there yet, but they're working on it.

What Google Does For Businesses

We provide a variety of tools to help businesses of all kinds succeed on and off the web. These programs form the backbone of our own business; they've also enabled entrepreneurs and publishers around the world to grow theirs. Our advertising programs, which range from simple text ads to rich media ads, help businesses find customers, and help publishers make money off of their content. We also provide cloud computing tools for businesses that save money and help organizations are more productive.

What Google Does For the Web

They build products that they hope will make the web better and therefore your experience on the web better. With products like Chrome and Android, they want to make it simpler and faster for people to do what they want to online. They're also committed to the open web, so they're involved in various projects to make it easier for developers to contribute to the online ecosystem and move the web forward. The web has evolved enormously since Google first appeared on the scene, but one thing that hasn't changed is their belief in the endless possibilities of the Internet itself. [xxiv]

It really is a win for everybody! The Golden Rule is good for employees. It's good for clients. And it's good for investors. The Golden Rule really does work. That's the fundamentals of Ethics.

OBSERVATIONS FROM
THE RESPONSIBLE DIRECT SELLER™

"How would I like to be treated in this situation?"

What a great question to be able to ask yourself when you come up against a situation where you are unsure of how to do the "*right*" thing.

Could you imagine if your down-line actually used this same question under similar circumstances?

Once you have answered this question, I recommend asking the next question:

"What could I do, so that I give back more than I would wish to receive in this situation?"

Always looking to give back more is another strong relationship builder.

The adoption of the "*Golden Rule*" for you and your business is a no-brainer!

It is accepted by everyone, easily understood by everyone, poses a win-win philosophy, and will help you navigate through just about any situation.

CHAPTER 7
WHY THE ETHICAL "GOLD STANDARD"
BEGINS WITH YOU

As I am writing this book, the entire world is actually struggling to overcome a horrific financial crisis, as a consequence of numerous deficit problems. One of these deficit problems which happen to be highly relevant to this book is the significant deficit of leadership.

When we consider the United States of America as an example, the deficit of leadership hasn't been more obvious as compared to any other time in history.

Why is it that the United States of America is developing less capable leadership?

Most likely the problem can be traced back to how the United States of America currently educates its children.

Back in the day when the founding fathers of the United States of America were being raised, 90% of the educational push was of a moral, ethical, religious nature.

Nevertheless, by the 1950's the percentage of that same educational push was so tiny it couldn't end up being effectively measured.

If we were to look back at the United States of America in 1776, the population was somewhere around three million people, and yet such legendary leaders such as Washington, Madison, Jefferson, Hamilton, Adams, etc.., were created.

Jump ahead to today and the United States of America does not have any one equal to the men of that caliber with a population of 315,500,000+. These same problems exist in the large majority of countries around the world. xxv

A solid ethical education empowers an individual to help to make superior ethical decisions. Nevertheless, because very few people today have obtained such an educational framework, how is it possible to get started on the correct ethical path? Just how do you take something as extensive as the Golden Rule and then make it an integral part of your day-to-day ethical thinking?

A sensible way to begin would be to take into consideration exactly what our needs as human beings happen to be.

Therefore, why don't we begin with discussing precisely what causes men and women to end up being fulfilled and just what leads to us not being fulfilled. We need to understand the distinction between what is generally known as influence and what is generally known as drive.

Regardless of what we choose to do in everyday life, it comes with an emotional side to everything you and I do.

The majority of us make a big effort to disregard this, simply because we're attempting to get the task completed. However it is the component that not only fulfills all of us but fuels all of us as men and women. And unless you understand or know that fuel, unless you recognize that drive, then you'll continually be seeking to get the temporary burst of energy by means of self-discipline or concentration, however you'll never be in a place of just flow.

Where it simply occurs. Where it is simply automatic.

Let's drill down a bit deeper on this subject matter.

All human beings possess diverse desires; however we are all motivated by the exact same set of needs. Understanding the six human needs makes it possible for you to definitely turn on your internal motivator, discover all that you're capable of, and turn out to be genuinely fulfilled on a regular basis. But before we discuss those six needs, let's look at a way of categorizing our experiences.

HUMAN EXPERIENCE - THE FOUR CLASSES[xxvi]

1.   Most people typically consider a Class One experience as a "peak life experience." A Class One experience:

   a.   Feels very good,

   b.   Is very good for you,

   c.   Is very good for others, and

   d.   Will serve the greater good.

2.   The majority of men and women desire to steer clear of Class Two experiences. Understanding their concepts, however, leads us to the most pleasure, development, and fulfillment. The Class Two experience:

a.   Does not feel very good,

b.   Is very good for you,

c.   Is very good for others, and

d.   Will serve the greater good.

3.   Non-productive Class Three experiences tend to provide instant enjoyment; however, at some point they damage our own standard of living and supply us with the greatest pain. Drinking alcohol to excess would most definitely fit into this category. A Class Three experience:

a.   Feels very good,

b.   Is not very good for you,

c.   Is not very good for others, and

d.   Genuinely does Not Serve the Greater Good.

4.   Men and women frequently take pleasure in Class Four experiences as a consequence of pressure from peers, conditioning, or perhaps outdated belief systems. Cigarette smoking, as an example, typically doesn't feel good the very first time, however many men and women continue doing it. The Class Four experience is something that:

a.   Genuinely does not feel very good,

b.   Is not very good for you,

c.   It is not very good for others, and

d.   Does not serve the greater good.

Let me explain to you what I consider the key to a successful, happy, and fulfilling life. It's discovering how to transform Class Two Experiences directly into Class One Experiences, discovering how to take those items that don't really feel very good however really are very good for you, truly serve others, are very good for others and truly serve the greater good, and making them a Class One experience where it also feels very good for you.

Do you believe that if you possessed the capability to survey every person on the planet, that the survey would likely reveal that men and women around the world possess comparable problems?

Yet each one of these men and women reside in various areas of the world and possess diverse belief systems. You will discover diverse rules. They all would have diverse backgrounds and different experiences. Exactly how could they possibly possess similar problems?

Is it feasible that all human beings have the same needs?

OK, as crazy as it sounds, it may be possible. So why would they have the same problems?

Is it feasible that these particular needs are basically in turmoil and that's the reason why we have the challenge? Would God actually do this to us? No, it might help to make life much more intriguing, almost certainly help to make us need to grow more, most likely help to make us attempt to figure things out.

THE SIX HUMAN NEEDS[xxvii]

All men and women possess exactly the same problems due to the fact everyone has the same six human needs. These needs are generally peculiar, in that they are most often in conflict with each other. Serious problems can occur whenever we select harmful tools or vehicles to attempt to fulfill these needs. As an alternative, we are able to decide to set up brand new behaviours for fulfilling our needs which will shift us swiftly toward life mastery.

To be fulfilled, we must consistently meet these six human needs:

- Certainty/comfort

- Uncertainty/variety

- Significance

- Connection/love

- Growth

- Contribution

All human beings have the need for:

1. Certainty/Comfort

a.   For the majority of people, certainty equates to them surviving. We all require a level of certainty that the roof will hold over our heads, the floor holds underneath our feet, and that we are able to steer clear of discomfort and acquire enjoyment.

b.   Precisely how do we satisfy this requirement for certainty? Quite a few men and women make an effort to achieve it by grabbing items that cause them to become certain they can be comfortable: food, drugs, alcohol, or cigarettes. Other individuals find it by submersing themselves in their work or by attempting to control every little thing around them, their environment or other people. These situations are usually Class Three experiences [they may feel good for the moment but are not good for you, not good for those around you, and do not serve the greater good].

c.   Exactly how do you attempt to get certainty in your life? Eliminate a few of the ways you attempt to be certain you can be comfortable, steer clear of discomfort, and acquire enjoyment.

d.   Here's the contradiction, though. Whenever you feel completely certain, when situations are totally predictable, you satisfy this need and become bored. And so although we would like certainty, we concurrently would like a certain amount of...

2. Uncertainty/Variety

a.   Absolutely everyone needs variety, something unexpected, and a challenge to really feel completely alive as well as experience fulfillment. With an excessive amount of certainty, we are bored. Similarly, together with too much variety, we turn out to be very afraid and concerned.

b.   Men and women will certainly breach their values in order to meet their needs. Selecting unacceptable vehicles only results in discomfort.

c.   There is actually a fragile balance between both of these needs that really must be struck for all of us to really feel truly fulfilled. Most people need a level of certainty within their lives to fully appreciate the variety. A number of men and women choose destructive methods for getting variety, such as using drugs or alcohol to alter their emotional states or the way they feel. Other individuals select neutral vehicles, like watching movies. Still others use constructive vehicles, like stimulating dialogue and opportunities to learn.

d.   How do you try to get variety in your life? List some of the constructive ways you try to create surprise, challenges, and diversity in your life.

3.   Significance

a.   We all have a need for significance, the sense that we are distinctive in some manner, that our lives possess a special purpose or meaning. We can make an effort to satisfy this need through detrimental vehicles, for example, making ourselves unique by manufacturing and believing that we are better than everyone else or by developing extreme problems that set us apart. Medical science research has shown that some men and women have even created the subconscious capability to make themselves sick so that they can gain the nurturing consideration of other individuals. This would clearly be a Class Four experience.

b.   Some men and women create a uniqueness by simply earning more income, possessing more "toys," attending school and achieving more degrees, or dressing in a distinctive way and possessing a particular fashion sense. Quite a few decide to live lives of incredible service to others, a positive Class One experience that could feel as if it was a Class Two from time to time.

c.   Just how do you attempt to obtain significance in your life? List some of the things you do that cause you to feel distinctive, needed, satisfied, or perhaps significant.

d.   We all need to feel unique. However paradoxically, in order to really feel unique we have to separate ourselves from other people. If we were feeling completely unique, we feel different and separate, which violates our need for...

4. Connections and Love

a.   All men and women need to feel connected with themselves, as well as with others with whom they can share their love.

b.   In order to satisfy this need, you could join a group or a club that possesses a positive purpose. A number of people join gangs, which have negative applications but still provide that sense of connection. Quite a few people feel immediate connection by aligning with their creator and feeling like they're being guided. People will steal, take drugs, or drink excessive amounts of alcohol to be part of the group and feel a sense of connection. Other individuals will perform at an extraordinary level in order to be accepted, loved, or connected to a high-performance team.

c.   As with all six human needs, if you give consistently that which you wish to receive, you will tend to get it back from others.

d.   How do you try to get connection and love in your life? List some of the ways you try to feel connected to yourself, to others, to your creator.

e.   These first four needs are basic needs. The next two would be the primary needs that must be met for you to feel totally fulfilled as a person.

5. Growth

a.   Growth equals life. On this planet, everything that is alive is either growing or dying. It doesn't matter how much money you have, how many people acknowledge you, or what you have achieved... Unless you feel like you're growing, you'll be unhappy and unfulfilled. But you must also be able to experience the euphoria of meaningful...

6. Contribution

a.   We all have a deep need to go beyond ourselves and to live a life that serves the greater good. In the moments that we do this, we experienced true joy and fulfillment.

b.   Contributing not only to others but to ourselves is a meaningful action, for we cannot give to others that which we do not have. A balance of contributions to oneself and to others, especially unselfish contribution, is the ultimate secret to the joy that so many people wish to have in their lives.

c.   How do you try to get growth and contribution in your life? List some of the things you do to obtain the feeling that you are growing and contributing, to yourself, to others, to the world at large.

THE REASON WHY MOST PEOPLE LOVE OR HATE TO TRY AND DO THINGS

Therefore if these are generally our six human needs, if these are generally our goals, then what exactly have we discovered? Here's what we discovered. To begin with, you are able to satisfy these first four needs in detrimental approaches and therefore will feel somewhat satisfied. Sufficient enough that you will be not really happy, but you will be not discontented enough to change. And you will probably not be satisfied simply because you won't grow and contribute, which are the supreme, fundamental, crucial needs.

This means that, for example, you have access to certainty in your life simply by controlling everybody. And on a zero to ten scale, perhaps that feels like a Level 3 of enjoyment and satisfaction. Are you with me so far? After which if you go to significance, chances are you'll do it by way of tearing everybody else down, consequently making yourself feel more significant.

That behaviour may provide you with a Level 3 or a 4. And you could have connection and love by receiving compassion on a regular basis, or being demanding, and observing that men and women are generally responding to you and then calling that love, which we know deep down it isn't. These methods will not help you to grow, they're not going to trigger you to contribute, and as a consequence you will not be satisfied. This is actually a fairly frightening place in life. When you are performing everything you believe you are designed to do and you're accomplishing it all, and you're still not satisfied. Now you'll know why.

Do you get it? Boy, if you just find a few vehicles, a few of them that meet all your needs, you cannot believe it. You won't need to inspire yourself. You won't really need to get yourself venturing out there. You won't really need to get yourself, give your little push, and listen to your little pump-up CD's. You are able to listen to CD's to get educated, listen to CD's maybe to get entertained, maybe just to remind yourself of the issues. But you'll know what to do because the drive will be inside you.

And you know what? You already possess this in certain areas of your life. Take it into consideration. Where's there an area in your life where there's something you love to do that for you is effortless? I would be willing to bet that no less than four of these six human needs are satisfied with that activity, and in all probability all six.

What is Something You Absolutely Hate to Do?

Prior to answering the above mentioned question, think about something you love to do and ask yourself, on a scale from zero to ten, how satisfied am I by that with regards to just how much certainty do I experience feeling? When I contemplate doing that, just how much certainty do I have that I'll have enjoyment performing that task? Just how much certainty do I have that I'll have fun with it, that I'll have ease and comfort at the very least? That at a minimum you'll be capable of steering clear of discomfort?

And then go to variety. How much uncertainty, how much variety on a scale of zero to ten will I have by participating? How much is different? How much of this would make me feel a sense of significance or uniqueness or feeling needed? And how much of this will give me these feelings of connection and love? How much of this will give me growth on a zero to ten scale? Contribution? And again, if it's something you love to do, I promise you, under your current strategy for perceiving things, appreciating them, noticing them; under your current strategy for doing things, you feel fulfilled in all six categories.

Now bring to mind something you absolutely hate to try and do. What's something you attempt to avoid carrying out if you are able to? Some of you will probably say, *"Cleaning my house."*

Ok, so on a scale of zero to ten; what's your degree of certainty that'll provide you with enjoyment or relaxation? Probably something like negative two. To some people it's a complete waste of time. Most people absolutely hate cleaning their house. To some people it makes them uncomfortable, because they're wasting time, and other things they could be doing are not getting done because of it.

What's your own sense of variety in cleaning your house, on a scale of zero to ten? To some people it would still be a negative two. They feel absolutely no variety in cleaning. As far as they are concerned, it's the same house, the same crap; it's in the same place. It's boring.

What's your sense of significance cleaning your house? Significance? To some people there's no significance, so on a scale of zero to ten, it would be a zero.

How about connection and love? To some people it would be a zero.

Let's look at growth? These same people would probably say zero.

Lastly, how about contribution? Simple, zero.

It's not necessarily too difficult to figure out. But guess what? There are men and women, that if asked, *"Who here loves to clean their house?"* A number of men and women will raise their hands and say they love to clean their house. And do you know why that is great? Because we all want to hire them, right?

So, if these men and women were asked, *"Do you have a sense of certainty that you're going to have enjoyment when you clean your house?"* There response may be, *"Absolutely, because you know what? When everything else in my life is so stirred up, I go clean my house. I feel like I've control over it, I feel good about things, I feel happy. You know, part of it is I have time for myself. And I know I do a good job. And I'm certain I can do a good job. And I can complete it and get it done."*

Let's ask these men and women, *"Do you have a sense of variety from cleaning the house?"* The response may be, *"Well, of course I do. Every time you clean the house, you don't know what you're going to find. Your kids put something down where it does not belong. There is always something new in different places. Plus I often listen to CD's, so I'm hearing something different. I'm learning something while I'm cleaning."*

How about significance, *"Do you get significance from cleaning your house?"* They may answer, *"Yes, I do, because I do a better job than anybody else."*

How about connection and love, *"Do you get connection love from cleaning your house?"* The response may be, *"Yes, I do, because when I'm ironing, I pray for my children and I feel connected to them."*

How about growth, *"Do you really grow when you are cleaning the house?"* You may hear something like, *"Yes, because I listened to CD's, I think about different ideas, I ask myself questions. Plus I solve new problems in the house, new challenges. Of course, I'm growing."*

How about contribution, *"Do you get a feeling of contribution from cleaning your house?"* You may be surprised and hear, *"Absolutely, nobody else will do it, so I'm contributing. That also, by the way, makes me unique because no one else will do it."*

Now let's connect all this. I will provide you with a few good examples after which let's connect it to you. But to start with, think for just a moment. What is one thing you absolutely hate to do? What is something you hate to do, and ask yourself, "This one thing I hate to do or to be politically correct, I'd prefer other people do, what's my degree of certainty that I'll have enjoyment or at least avoid discomfort by doing this, that I will be comfortable doing this?" Zero to ten, precisely what is your degree of certainty it'll be enjoyable? I'd be inclined to wager it's fairly low, isn't it? Perhaps it's zero, possibly below? Then again, maybe it's two, three, or four.

Precisely what is your sense of positive variety of a zero to ten scale? That there will be positive surprises or differences in this activity? Probably one of the reasons you don't like doing it is you don't see there's much variety. To you it is the same old thing. Some other people enjoy it because they see variety in it, but you don't. Zero to ten? Yeah, you're probably in that minus level, one, two, in that range. Right?

Consider significance? This specific thing you hate to do. Exactly how significant does it help you feel? How important do you feel? Unique when you're doing this? My guess is pretty low or a zero.

What about the sense of connection and love when you do it? Consider it a moment. How connected. How much love do you experience feeling doing this thing you hate to do? My guess is pretty darn low again.

How about growth? You might go, *"Yeah, I grow doing it."* No. I don't mean do you grow. I said when you think about doing it, how much growth do you associate to it? Probably very little.

And again, contribution? You go, *"Yeah, I contribute."* Again, I don't want to know if you contribute. I want to know does it feel, when you think about doing this; do you feel like you're contributing? Now many times you do contribute but you don't give yourself credit so that's why it doesn't feel fulfilling.

Does this make sense to you? Anything in life can be totally fulfilling if you know what the goal of the game is. All you need to do is organize the game to meet it.

So, now you are a little more aware of how we classify our experiences, as well as the depth of the six human needs.

Now with this knowledge the six human "*macro*" needs, let's focus our attention on the Direct Selling Professional and their "*micro*" needs...

ADOPTING THE ETHICAL "GOLD STANDARD"

Exactly how should we as Direct Selling Professionals commence the adoption of this Ethical Guideline?

Just how do you take something as wide-ranging as the Golden Rule and help to make it an integral part of your day-to-day thinking?

Begin with this question:

How Would I as A Direct Selling Professional Want To Be Treated?

I have faith that all Direct Selling Professionals, at their core, are very much alike.

Below is a condensed list of things which I believe that virtually all men and women share with regards to the way they wish to be treated:

As A Direct Selling Professional, I Truly Would Like To Be Valued

Are you aware that within the United States Economic marketplace of the past 20 years, over 70% of men and women leave their day jobs, and do so because they do not feel valued by their company?[xxviii]

What percentage of these men and women is part of the Direct Selling Profession?

Let us run some quick numbers. The population of the United States of America at the printing of this book was 315,500,000+.[xxix]

So 70% of the population would equal 220,850,000+.

What if only 25% of the 70% (220,850,000+) where part of the Direct Selling Profession, how many fellow direct sellers are impacted with the feeling of be undervalued?

Answer: 5,521,250+ men and women

There isn't a Direct Selling Professional around the world that doesn't desire to be valued by others. Wouldn't you desire other individuals to simply accept you for who you really are and demonstrate through their daily actions that you matter and make a difference?

Most people have experienced the feeling of being worthless as a result of another person's actions. See if the list below reminds you of anyone.

Perhaps a school teacher or even a whole lot worse a parent or guardian who informed you that you as an individual have absolutely nothing to offer this world.

Your employer or supervisor announced that you and your division is really a financial drain on the company.

Some individual made the decision that it would most likely end up being amusing to publicly humiliate you.

If anyone of the three hits home, then you already know precisely how essential it is to be valued by another human being.

In the Direct Selling Profession, inspiration is like oxygen; it is far better to have it than not to have it.

I am of the belief that deep down, just about all Direct Selling Professionals desire to feel that they matter simply for who they are.

This is basically the idea regarding the valuing of others. The cornerstone of the Golden Rule is to value others for who they are as human beings and not what they can do for us or what position they may hold in the real world.

In the event that you truly understand this concept, then you are well on your way to making the Golden Rule your ethical compass.

As A Direct Selling Professional, I Truly Wish to Be Appreciated

The desire to end up being cherished and valued could very well be number one need of every Direct Selling Professional.

The second greatest need would most likely be our desire to be appreciated for our effort and hard work. All Direct Selling Professionals possess the desire to succeed and accomplish great things.

It's fair to say that you want to be appreciated for the expertise and hard work you bring to your organization and personal life. So, if you happen to be at all like me, it is very important to recognize that what you do actually matters in the larger scheme of things and helps develop your self-confidence and personal self-worth.

Why compare yourself with others? No one in the entire world can do a better job of being you than you.

Here are four ways to start the process of appreciation:

Start by making an effort to communicate to other Direct Selling Professionals that you personally appreciate their particular efforts.

Say thanks to them at each and every chance.

Offer credit to others every time you can.

Make it a point to praise direct sellers in the presence of those closest to them, such as family members.

As A Direct Selling Professional I Truly Wish To Be Trusted

It could very well be said that trust is the foundation of all good relationships. Whether it is a marriage, business relationships, or a friendship, all require trust. In the event that you don't have trust, there can never be any open or honest interaction, and most likely that particular relationship will be only temporary.

The list below contains some of the best ways that a Direct Selling Professional can build trust with others:

- Display compassion on a consistent basis

- Preserve your own integrity

- Retain those things that you hold in confidence from others

- Concentrate upon mutual objectives as opposed to personal itineraries

- Always listen with an open mind

- Demonstrate respect for your up line, your down line, your customers, as equivalent associates

- Carry out what's right, irrespective of personal risk

- Freely and honestly communicate vision and values

"A good marriage is at least 80 percent good luck in finding the right person at the right time. The rest is trust." - Nanette Newman

It's going to take a leap of faith to place your trust in another individual, especially someone you don't know very well. Nevertheless, that's what must be done to put into practice the Golden Rule. Ironically, nurturing a new Direct Selling Professional requires a similar leap of faith on your part.

As A Direct Selling Professional, I Truly Wish To Be Respected

Anytime that another person places trust in you, you actually acquire accountability as well as recognition. Whenever others respect you, it will touch something much deeper within you. This trust placed in you will provide you with dignity, and it will help build your self-confidence.

"Thought cannot avoid the ethical or reverence and love for all life. It will abandon the old confined systems of ethics and be forced to recognize the ethics that knows no bounds. But on the other hand, those who believe in love for all creation must realize clearly the difficulties involved in the problem of a boundless ethic and must be resolved not to veil from [humankind] the conflicts, which this ethic will involve [us], but allow [us] really to experience them. To think out in every implication the ethic of love for all creation -- this is the difficult task, which confronts our age. "- Albert Schweitzer

10 RULES FOR RESPECT

1. If you have a problem with me, come to me (privately).

2. If I have a problem with you, I'll come to you (privately).

3. If someone has a problem with me and comes to you, send them to me. (I'll do the same for you.)

4. If someone consistently will not come to me, say, "Let's go to the pastor together. I am sure he will see us about this." (I will do the same for you.)

5. Be careful how you interpret me—I'd rather do that. On matters that are unclear, do not feel pressured to interpret my feelings or thoughts. It is easy to misinterpret intentions.

6. I will be careful how I interpret you.

7. If it's confidential, don't tell. (This especially applies to board meetings.) If you or anyone comes to me in confidence, I won't tell unless (a) the person is going to harm himself/herself, (b) the person is going to physically harm someone else, © a child has been physically or sexually abused. I expect the same from you.

8. I do not read unsigned letters or notes.

9. I do not manipulate; I will not be manipulated; do not let others manipulate you. Do not let others try to manipulate me through you. I will not preach "at" you on Sunday mornings. I will leave conviction to the Holy Spirit (he does it better anyway).

10. When in doubt, just say it. The only dumb questions are those that don't get asked. We are a family here and we care about each other, so if you have a concern, pray, and then (if led) speak up. If I can answer it without misrepresenting something or breaking a confidence, I will. xxx

As A Direct Selling Professional, I Wish To Be Understood

At times, a Direct Selling Professional's issue is brought on by yet another individual's callousness or perhaps indifference. However, by and large, the difficulty develops from a lack of knowledge. It's humorous the way we can be fast to find fault with other people when they don't adjust to the behaviour or criteria we hold. However when we take the time to get to know them, we quite often realize that their approach isn't the wrong way, it's just a different way.

When dealing with other individuals, we as Direct Selling Professionals should seek first to understand, then to be understood. That requires a mindset of overall flexibility along with a desire to be teachable.

I have heard it be said that love is saying *'I feel differently'* instead of *'you're wrong.'*

As A Direct Selling Professional, I Truly Do Not Want Others to Take Advantage of Me

On the subject of how others treat me, above all else I don't want anyone to take advantage of me. That's truly the main point here with regards to ethical behavior. The majority of us don't have to straighten out complex philosophical challenges or ethical riddles. If men and women could decipher that I am taking advantage of them (even though I've had an opportunity to make clear my objectives) then my actions are in all probability an awful idea.

There exists a revealing account about Marvin Bower, the renowned leader of McKinsey & Co. who died on Jan. 22, 2003 at age 99. The story affirms a lot concerning the foundational values of this humble man, who was simply referred to as the father of management consulting.

In the 1950s, Bower was requested to visit Los Angeles by then billionaire Howard Hughes, who wanted him to analyze Paramount Pictures. Throughout the visit, Hughes was in a benevolent disposition and drove the new consultant around in his ancient Chevrolet, even offering him a late-night tour of the Spruce Goose, the enormous wooden plane Hughes developed during the war.

However Bower believed that absolutely nothing good could possibly come of working for Hughes. He found the entrepreneur's method of business "so unorthodox and so unusual" that he believed he would never be able to help Paramount. Instead of taking the assignment and reaping a big fee, he walked away.

The move ended up being classic Bower. He built McKinsey into a global consulting powerhouse by making it mandatory that values mattered more than money. He extolled the idea that consulting was not a business but a profession, arguing that, like the best doctors and lawyers, consultants should put the interests of their clients first, conduct themselves ethically, and insist on telling clients the truth, not what they wanted to hear.

That was as unusual then as it is today. But so was Bower, a towering figure at McKinsey and in the larger world of consulting. At McKinsey, Bower helped to move consulting from shop-floor efficiency studies to major strategy reviews for top-tier corporations. He created one of the world's most productive leadership factories, producing hundreds of corporate CEOs and presidents. [xxxi]

UNDERSTANDING THE VALUE OF PEOPLE

A number of companies in the United States are relearning this lesson. They are rediscovering the value of valuing people. Plus they are generating internal corporate changes to help market the good treatment of their employees to the marketplace. One particular company is Starbucks. So, what makes Starbucks so great? Partners at the coffee seller told us, *"I love that we can receive benefits and stock rewards at 20 hours/week"* and *"There is potential for anyone to move up the ladder."* [xxxii]

Successful organizations place men and women first, invest in their development and provide them with the tools, training and support they need to be successful. This results not just in bottom line success, but lower attrition rates and high levels of creativeness, innovation and excellence.

Microsoft, Motorola, W.L. Gores & Associates, Southwest Airlines, Ben & Jerry's, Homemade, Hewlett-Packard, Lincoln Electric and Starbuck's pursue "people-first" strategies.

Evidence demonstrates that successful organizations put men and women first. Personnel are a company's only genuine competitive advantage. Competitors can match up with most organization's products, processes, locations, distribution channels and so on.

Precisely what methods distinguish people first organizations?

- Cultural diversity

- Family-friendly

- Investing in employee training

- Empowering their employees

Consequently, this converts into higher employee efficiency and fulfillment. These employees are prepared to put forth the extra effort to carry out whatever is necessary to see that their jobs are done properly and completely.

People-first strategies also lead to organizations being able to recruit smarter, more conscientious, and more loyal employees.

STARBUCKS - SUCCESSFUL ORGANIZATION PUT PEOPLE FIRST

Company Background

Founded by Jerry Baldwin, Zev Siegel, and Gordon Bowker in 1971 in Seattle's Pike Place Market.

Purchased by Howard Schultz in March 1987 and turned into what we see today.

Schultz wanted to create a business that does the right things for the right reasons and is financially successful.

Mission Statement

Establish Starbucks as the premier purveyor of the finest coffee in the world while maintaining our uncompromising principles while we grow.

Guiding Principles

To support their mission statement the following six guiding principles help guide the appropriateness of decisions:

- Provide a great work environment and treat each other with respect and dignity.

- Embrace diversity as an essential component in the way we do business.

- Apply the highest standards of excellence to the purchasing, roasting and fresh delivery of our coffee.

- Develop enthusiastically satisfied customers all of the time.

- Contribute positively to our communities and our environment.

- Recognize the profitability is essential to our success.

Putting "*people first*" is easy to say. Putting people first is not necessarily consistent with long term competitiveness. Organizations are more typically pursuing a "*labour cost minimization*" strategy rather than a people-first strategy. As a result most firms place profits over people.

Organizations with problems typically look to staffing cuts as a first response. Few organizations have the luxury to be able to provide workers with anything more than minimal job security. Employees are a variable cost.

Learning from Starbucks

Starbucks is one of the most successful and admired companies today. It has grown from a single coffee shop in Seattle 42 years ago to an $11.7 billion international company. From tasty beverages to proprietary whole bean coffee blends to strategic relationships, small businesses have so much to learn from Starbucks.

10 Lessons

More than the taste of its coffee, there are a number of factors that propelled Starbucks' latte to the forefront. Below are some of the things that you can learn from Starbucks, a company that started small, dreamed big and grew to be a gigantic global corporation.

1. Start with a good business concept

2. Think big

3. Think outside the box

4. Partner big

5. Create a unique experience

6. Keep customers happy

7. Dig deep into customer's wallet

8. Roll out new initiatives

9. Practice good management

10. Diversified your revenue stream

And just what are we able to gain from Starbucks in regard to putting people first? That's simple. To treat others as they want to be treated. Whenever a man or women has a good sense of how he or she wants to be treated, with dignity, respect, understanding, and trust, then he or she can easily figure out how to treat others.

OBSERVATIONS FROM
THE RESPONSIBLE DIRECT SELLER™

How can you implement the Golden Rule?

You first have to take your eyes off yourself, permanently, and focus them on what is right for others!

When we build an organization, we must ensure that the direct sellers that get involved in our business feel that they are a valued asset to our organization.

How can we do that? There are a number of ways, but continually communicating with them about their success and that you are there to help them reach what they define as success will go a long way to making them feel valued.

The same goes for feeling appreciated. We all want to feel appreciated.

Think of how your up-line makes you feel appreciated. If for some reason they don't, do one of two things: (1) look a little higher up, or (2) decide how you would like to be appreciated and ensure that you focus that down-line.

Respect is easy when you use the Golden Rule. Everyone deserves to be respected as human beings. End of story.

If you feel differently, get out of the Direct Selling Profession; you are a cancer!

Remember when you first decided to get involved in direct selling? What were two things that you wanted to make sure happened?

Mine were the following:

- Not to have anyone take advantage of me, and

- Have someone understand my current position.

These two concerns are actually easy to overcome. However, they are continuously being measured. To be clear:

I remember being told by an up-line within one of my businesses when I first started, that unless I trusted them from the beginning, they wouldn't work with me.

This same individual suggested that my current situation wasn't important to them as it pertained to how they mentor, as they "*coach*" everyone the same way.

Do you see a problem with these two statements? If not, you should be concerned!

Working with direct sellers is not always easy, but one of the ways to make it easier is to continually work to ensure that these two concerns are being met.

CHAPTER 8
HOW TO LIVE THE "GOLD STANDARD" AT THE HIGHEST LEVEL

It is only a man or woman of character who can influence others. Character is paramount to living a lifetime of integrity and ethical excellence.

As A Direct Selling Professional, Character Is Much More Than Speaking

A lot of Direct Selling Professionals speak about carrying out what's right, however action is definitely the true measure of character.

"If you will think about what you ought to do for other people, your character will take care of itself. Character is a by-product, and any man who devotes himself to its cultivation in his own case will become a selfish prig." - Woodrow Wilson

As A Direct Selling Professional, Talent Is Really a Gift - Character Is Really a Decision

There are plenty of things in life you don't get to select, such as where you're born, who your parents are, and how tall you are. But there are some critical things every person does select. We select our faith, our attitude, and our character.

As A Direct Selling Professional, Character Delivers Long Lasting Achievement

Trust is vital when working with people. Character begets trust.

As A Direct Selling Professional, You Are Unable To Exceed the Restrictions of Your Character

- There are really only three kinds of Direct Selling Professionals:

- Direct Selling Professionals who never succeed;

- Direct Selling Professionals who achieve success only temporarily; and

- Direct Selling Professionals who become and remain successful.

- Possessing character is definitely the only sure way to sustain success. Regardless of how skilled or rich or attractive a Direct Selling Professional is, they're not going to have the ability to outrun their character.

If you wish to live a character-filled life which demonstrates ethical superiority, follow these guidelines. They will assist you to incorporate the Golden Rule into the essence of your life:

1. Embrace This Guideline as the Integrity Compass for Your Life

Nobody wants to end up being an echo, to live a shadow of a life. However that is frequently the destiny of men and women without beliefs. In the event you want your life to have meaning, then you definitely must select some basic principle to live by.

Previously I've made the case for the Golden Rule. As I've said, asking the question, "*How would I like to be treated in this situation?*" is an excellent integrity guideline for just about any situation. It works in your organization, meeting new prospects, training your down line, and in your home. It works with up line, down line, family and friends. It works whether you're leading an organization of one or an organization of tens of thousands.

If you believe the Golden Rule is right and it works, then you need to adopt it as the integrity compass for your life. Every single day, whenever the matter of ethical conduct comes up with you, ask this question: "*How would I like to be treated in this situation?*"

By keeping genuine, do not be embarrassed about carrying out the right thing, and choose what you believe is correct and stay with it.

2. Make Your Choices According To This Integrity Guideline

The majority of people make only a couple of critical decisions in life and from that point manage those decisions daily. As soon as you choose to make the Golden Rule the integrity guideline for your life, you might want to reconsider some of your previous decisions. Such as:

Exactly how will the Golden Rule alter my goals?

Will I interact differently with my family?

Will I need to alter the way I approach my career? (Some direct sellers feel obligated to change jobs because their work environment is adverse to Golden Rule living.)

I once had an up line that told me, *"Kevin, to know and not to do, is not to know."* I always remembered that line.

Remember, the more substantial the decision, the greater the courage it could possibly require.

Carrying out what's right when it is uncomfortable to do so is absolutely no minor thing. However the benefits are enormous.

While you apply the Golden Rule to your life and make decisions based on it, keep in mind the following:

Choices, And Certainly Not Circumstances, Determine Your Own Integrity: men and women of weak character have a tendency to blame their choices on conditions. People of ethics make good choices irrespective of conditions. In the event that they make sufficient good choices, they start to create much better circumstances for themselves.

Incorrect Decisions Leave Behind Emotional Disfigurements: each and every time men and women make incorrect decisions, there is definitely an impact, regardless of whether they immediately recognize it or not.

The Greater Amount Of People Included, The Greater The Stress With Regard To Complying: moral choices made in private have their own stress, simply because some people might be inclined to believe that a private indiscretion won't ever turn out to be public knowledge. Public decisions connected with other men and women possess a different kind of stress, that of complying. No matter how much stress there is, you simply can't permit other individuals to pressure you into creating unethical decisions.

Idleness Is Also A Choice: some men and women's response to ethical decision-making is to steer clear of taking action. Nevertheless, it's essential to keep in mind that idleness is also a decision. Unfortunately, for every one individual willing to stand-up and point out their organization's ethical transgressions, there are millions of men and women who decide every single day not to take action when they observe their organization take shortcuts or compromise ethics, and to inevitably live with the consequences.

To live a life of integrity and ethics, you will need to maintain your principles while you make tough decisions.

Basic principles, especially moral principles, can never be at the mercy of the wind. A moral principle is a compass forever fastened and forever true, and that is as essential in your business as it is in your home.

3. Control Your Choices In Accordance With This Particular Integrity Guideline

With regards to ethics, at times it is easy to make the substantial decisions. The majority of people don't have a very hard time making the conscious decision to not take someone's life. A handful of men and women are inclined to perform "*grand theft auto*" or "*breaking and entering*." Nevertheless, the minor things can be difficult to control. There's an old saying, "*god is in the details.*" You can also say ethics is in the details.

You will discover three primary questions for ethical decision-making:

- Is what I am about to do legal?

- Is what I am about to do balanced?

- How will what I am about to do make me feel about myself?

To generally be considered trustworthy, you need to be predictable. When you control your life and all the decisions (minor or major) by a single principle, the Golden Rule, you develop an ethical predictability in your own life. Men and women are going to have confidence in you, understanding that you consistently do the right thing.

4. Request Other Individuals to Hold You Accountable For Your Actions

Has another man or woman at any time stood looking over your shoulder while you labored on a task? If that's the case, the chances are pretty good that you didn't enjoy it. The majority of men and women do not appreciate being micromanaged. In addition to being micromanaged for everyday tasks, men and women appreciate it even less when another person checks up on them to make certain that they are being truthful and dependable. Nevertheless, it is precisely what I would recommend that you do if you would like to live by the Golden Rule, simply because absolutely nothing assists a person to be honest like accountability.

It really is interesting. Most people don't especially like to be reminded of our own weak points, and we don't especially like our weak points revealed to others either. However if we want to grow, we will need to deal with the pain of disclosing our own actions to others. Integrity is the basic foundation of a person's life, and accountability is the cornerstone. It provides teeth to our commitment to live by high ethical standards.

THE GOLDEN RULE AND THE LIFE OF J.C. PENNEY

Any time you study the lives of great men and women, you can actually tell any time one of these "*special people*" has lived their life based on the Golden Rule. Among my favorites is the story of J.C. Penney, the founding father of the department stores that display his name. The son of a farmer, James Cash (J.C.) Penney was raised in Hamilton, Missouri. His father started developing J.C. Penney's character early on, teaching him about the marketplace, self-sufficiency, and the Golden Rule. An interesting example of this started when J.C. Penney was 8 years old, he was expected to earn enough money to purchase his own clothes.

To earn money, J.C. Penney labored and scraped together $2.50 to buy a young piglet. Subsequently he performed house chores for the surrounding neighbors so that he could gather slops for the piglet in order to fatten it up. When J.C. Penney sold it during slaughter season, he earned a good profit. Observing the key benefits of such an arrangement, he bought a dozen piglets the next season, and he gathered corn from the farms rows after the huskers were finished harvesting. The pigs were growing nicely, and J.C. Penney expected to make a great profit in the fall. However on one particular day his father forced him to sell them simply because the neighbors were protesting and complaining about the smell. J.C. Penney commented, "*It was the off-season for pork... But my father lived by the Golden Rule in relation to his neighbors, and it was important to him for me to see that I should too.*" xxxiii

As J.C. Penney got older, he discovered that he had a talent for purchasing and selling, and he constantly labored at it. At the same time his father encouraged him and made sure he was always scrupulously honest. He also assisted his son to get his first job in a dry goods store in Hamilton, Missouri. There J.C. Penney learned his trade. In time he managed to move on to other stores, always working hard and treating others as he wanted to be treated. At one store in particular, when he learned that the same socks were priced several different ways in order to take advantage of unwitting customers, he resigned. Eventually he got on with a store whose owners invited him to become a partner. He was so good at his trade; the men offered him a partnership in additional stores they intended to open. And when the original owners wanted to leave the business in 1907, J.C. Penney bought them out.

J.C. Penny had a vision for a chain of stores all across the western United States. His strategy was to discover trustworthy, diligent men and teach them his approach to business. And in the event that they succeeded in managing their store well and turned around and trained another man to do the same, he would offer them partnership in a new store, just as it had been offered to him. *"I think, if we pick the right kind of men and train them the right way, they will all catch the spirit of partnership idea,"* he told the first manager he invited to become part owner of the store. xxxiv

And what were those original stores called? He named them for his philosophy of business. They were called the Golden Rule stores, "hence," explained J.C. Penney, *"in setting up a business under the name and meaning? Of the Golden Rule, I was publicly binding myself, in my business relations, to a principle which had been a real and intimate part of my family upbringing. To me the sign in the store was much more than the trade name."* xxxv

Though J.C. Penney later changed the names on the stores when his organization incorporated during expansion, he never stopped living, and working, by the Golden Rule, putting partnership ahead of profits. He stated his philosophy succinctly: *"money is properly the by-product of building men as partners."* xxxvi

J.C. Penney continued to work and create partners for many years. He finally turned the business over to one of the people he'd made a partner, a man who'd worked for him in one of the first stores. J.C. Penney lived by the Golden Rule, treating others with respect, giving them value in business, and providing the best merchandise he could procure. He lived to be 95 years old.

There's a classic saying that when you get squeezed, whatever is in you will come out. That makes sense and I believe that is true. However I also understand that an individual is unable to develop a Golden Rule life overnight. J.C. Penney was blessed. His parents trained him in the Golden Rule from infancy, and he embraced it all his life. If you've had that kind of upbringing, thank your parents. If you haven't, it's still not too late to change.

OBSERVATIONS FROM
THE RESPONSIBLE DIRECT SELLER™

You have decided to build an international business, so you now have a significant responsibility to everyone with whom you interact.

As I've mentioned before, it all starts with you. Begin by evaluating your own character.

Character – and not your circumstances – should determine your decisions.

We must take responsibility for everything we do, and STOP blaming others or circumstances for anything.

Circumstances may interfere with our lives or our business, but it is how we control our attitude about these circumstances that is important.

Remember: any wrong decisions you make in your business will have a negative impact not only on your business, but also on the direct sellers above and below you!

By the way, doing nothing is not an option. Neither is quitting.

You decided to start, so finish what you started.

Use your up-line mentor to hold you accountable.

If your mentor does his/her job, they will tell you what you need to hear and not what you want to hear.

If that is not what is happening, fire your mentor and find someone who will coach you properly.

CHAPTER 9
WHAT TO WATCH OUT FOR WHEN
ADOPTING THE "GOLD STANDARD"

Sabotaging the Golden Rule

Carrying out what's right really does receive a great deal of consideration nowadays. How come? Simply because it's actually news whenever somebody practices the Golden Rule, encounters unfavorable implications for it and is happy that he did what's right.

Let's face the facts; there are numerous issues that encourage men and women to cross an ethical line. As I've worked alongside men and women and led organizations for more than 28 years, I actually have regrettably witnessed lots of people compromise their own standards. And I can tell you that having worked with men and women in just about every socioeconomic group in more than 42 countries around the world, in my opinion it always comes down to one of 5 aspects. The following are the five aspects that most frequently come up whenever an individual compromises his / her ethics:

Aspect #1 – Pressure

The majority of the ethical violations which keep mounting within the global marketplace and government today result from senior executives and political leaders covering up the real truth. They do it to make their organizations or administrations appear more successful than they really are.

A recent study by the Ethics Resource Center of Washington revealed:

Study: Ethical breaches becoming common in government.

"A new report suggests that a crisis in principles and morals is looming in government and may even be under way... 'While government misconduct is high, it's likely to get worse,'... 'We believe that the next Enron could take place in the public sector. At present, government lacks many of the important interventions that could reduce this risk.'

... 52 percent of government employees reported witnessing some kind of misconduct by co-workers in 2006[This study is now 7 years old – is

there any update, or more recent data?]... 23 percent said they saw or experienced abusive behavior, 21 percent witnessed safety violations and 20 percent knew someone who had lied to their colleagues or was involved in a possible conflict of interest.

Most reports of misconduct involved ethical breaches, rather than legal violations, according to ERC.

Government employees as a whole reported 3 percent more incidents of falsifying or altering documents and 4 percent more incidents of lying to employees than their private sector counterparts did.

... misconduct was up 12 percent from 2005, from 58 percent to 70 percent. 'It's very likely that higher levels of management are unaware that misconduct is even a problem within their organization'...

... 25 percent of employees saying they worked in situations that were conducive to wrongdoing and 48 percent saying they encountered situations that invited unethical behavior.

'The public trusts that government leaders have strong ethics and make sure they're followed throughout their organizations.... In setting standards, the government must look at itself." [xxxvii]

Within our fast-paced lifestyle, there's no doubt that just about everybody feels some type of pressure. Along with pressure comes the enticement to take short-cuts or out and out lie. Publicly-traded corporations have senior executives that feel pressure to improve their respective stock price. Direct Selling Professionals feel pressure to generate much more sales. Students feel pressure to obtain better grades. Not one person escapes the pressure. Therefore the real question is: How are you going to deal with the pressure?

Because you encounter daily pressure, watch out for how you could possibly be influenced to compromise your values, and ask yourself some tough questions:

As a Direct Selling Professional, should I make hasty emotionally charged decisions?

Pressure generates anxiety, and anxiety can certainly create emotionally charged moments for some Direct Selling Professionals. Some Direct Selling Professionals have difficulty in these circumstances, and they end up making very poor decisions that impact themselves and/or their down line. How can I as a Direct Selling Professional guard against that?

As a Direct Selling Professional, should I compromise the simple truth?

Some Direct Selling Professionals find it nearly impossible to confess to making an error. Am I as a Direct Selling Professional prepared to adhere to the truth regardless of whether I don't like it?

As a Direct Selling Professional, should I cut corners?

It has been said that the longest distance between two points is a short-cut. While that may be true, pressure tempts us as Direct Selling Professionals to contemplate short cuts when we in any other case wouldn't. Am I as a Direct Selling Professional prepared to battle to carry out what's right?

As a Direct Selling Professional, should I maintain my personal obligations?

Men and women in direct selling are identical in their promises. However, it is only in their exploits that they differ. Am I as a Direct Selling Professional likely to continue to keep my promise as well as follow through, regardless of whether it hurts or not?

As a Direct Selling Professional, should I bend to the opinions of others?

Some direct sellers tend to be particularly vulnerable to the opinions of others. That was true of me for the first 15 years of my direct selling involvement. Will I as a Direct Selling Professional carry out the things I realize are right, regardless of whether it's popular or unpopular?

As a Direct Selling Professional, should I make commitments I can't preserve?

"We ought not to raise expectations which it is not in our power to satisfy. It is more pleasing to see smoke brighten into flame, than flame sinking into smoke." - Samuel Johnson.

How am I as a Direct Selling Professional planning to maintain my commitments from going up in flames?

In case your objective is always to make good decisions under pressure, I would recommend that you might want reminders of exactly what's at stake. First, keep in mind that you happen to be accountable to God. Second, keep in mind that you happen to be accountable to your family. I personally keep reminders of that around me all the time. On my laptop, the background picture is of my wife and daughter so I'll never forget that people are depending on me to do right. One of my definitions of success is for those family, friends and colleagues that are closest to me to love and respect me the most.

Memory joggers tend to be invaluable, however they are insufficient. Furthermore, I require systems to help keep me personally on track. For example, if I need to come to a decision under pressure, I most certainly will spend some time to write out the problem and solution so I won't behave rashly. I take note of promises I make thus so that I can easily remember them. I additionally use software on my laptop and Smartphone to follow up with me on decisions and promises in order that they don't slip through the cracks. I would recommend that you do similar types of things. Do whatever you must to maintain your ethics under pressure.

Aspect #2 – Pleasure

The reality is that the pleasures the majority of us engage in are generally short-lived and leave us unsatisfied. The things which induce us infrequently deliver on what they promise.

Exactly what is the answer to the enticement of pleasure? Perhaps, the first thought should be to run quickly from enticement.

If you understand you happen to be particularly vulnerable to a certain pleasure that is going to induce you to cross an ethical line, run in the opposite direction. Whenever you observe it approaching, stop and change direction and remove yourself from that enticement. The most effective way to steer clear of enticement is to prevent it in the first place.

The second solution is to develop discipline.

"Discipline is the screw, the nail, the cement, the glue, the nut, the bolt, the rivet that holds everything tight. Discipline is the wire, the connecting rod, and the chain that coordinates. Discipline is the oil that makes machines run fast, and the oil that makes parts slide smooth, as

well as the oil that makes the metal bridge. They know about discipline here. The principle of discipline here is divinely simple; you lay it on thick and fast, all the time." - Private Gerald Kersh

It's interesting, but to achieve independence, you will need to contain your emotional behavior with discipline. That requires character. One of the simplest ways to develop discipline is usually to postpone pleasure.

The current generation doesn't accomplish that at all. We are in an "I want it now" culture. If you require further proof, take a look at "real-time" Debt Statistics at www.USDebtClock.org – WARNING – This page may scare you a bit if you are concerned about the debt of the United States of America.

- Total Personal Debt: $15.9 Trillion

- Mortgage Debt: $13.1 Trillion

- Student Loan Debt: $979 Billion

- Credit Card Debt: $849 Billion

- National Debt: $16.8 Trillion [xxxviii]

The concepts of delayed versus instant pleasure are undoubtedly one of the most important choices that separate rich thinking from poor thinking. And it isn't a choice until you've consciously identified it as one. Since it's too often a matter of unconscious repeating of the pattern that your family or closest friends are instilling in you, it's very important to think it through for yourself. Does no money down with fixed monthly payments really make more sense to you compared to acquiring assets that pay for what you want? Your answer should address both financial and emotional sensibility.

Direct Selling leaders who have lost their minds to pleasure and possessions sadly help to make themselves untrustworthy to their up line and down line. Any Direct Selling Professional who actually enjoys pleasure more than truth is actually on course for difficulty, and will unfortunately take his / her down line with them.

Aspect #3 – Power

The majority of the latest scandals in American business have been the result of senior executives abusing the power of their positions. These misguided people started to believe that the actual assets of the publicly traded companies they led could possibly be dealt with as their own personal property. Unfortunately, for many Direct Selling Professionals, having power is like drinking salt water. The more you drink, the thirstier you get.

Enron and WorldCom have since become a popular symbol of willful corporate fraud and corruption. The scandals were also considered landmark cases in the field of business fraud and brought into question the ethical practices of many corporations throughout the United States.

Direct Selling Professionals who happen to be particularly vulnerable to power issues typically experience a cycle that follows the following pattern:

The Acquisition of Power: Power itself is fairly neutral, similar to money. It's a device which can be used for good or ill. However it can be very dangerous, especially for Direct Selling Professionals who become successful quickly and obtain power previous to being ready for it.

The Misuse of Power: One of many dangers associated with power for a Direct Selling Professional is the fact that those who find themselves trusted with it start to make its upkeep their own main objective. These Direct Selling Professionals don't seem to understand or know that the power that they've been granted, regardless of whether it's in their business, community, friends, or family, has been bestowed on them for the purpose of service. Those Direct Selling Professionals who seem to want most to maintain their power no matter what are in all likelihood to compromise typical ethical behavior to maintain it.

The Deprivation of Power: Unsurprisingly, any Direct Selling Professional who actually abuses their power will lose their power. Abusive Direct Selling Professionals, like dictators, are living on borrowed time.

Power is similar to a grand waterway. Provided that it maintains its course, it is a beneficial masterpiece of design. However when it floods its banks, it usually brings amazing devastation. How does a Direct Selling Professional maintain power in its banks? Perhaps we could take a page out of the 33rd President of the United States of America, Harry S. Truman. He recommended, *"If a man can accept a situation in a place of power with the thought that it's only temporary, he comes out all right. But when he thinks he is the cause of the power that can be his ruination."* Any Direct Selling Professional who knows that they are safeguarding their power excessively ought to begin evaluating themselves for breaches of ethics. Power can be horribly seductive.

<u>Aspect #4 – Pride</u>

You may possibly not instantly consider pride as a prospective trap that could weaken ethics as well as work against the practice of the Golden Rule. All things considered, aren't men and women admonished to take pride in their job? Don't most people encourage their own children's good behaviour simply by letting them know exactly how proud they are of them? Aren't students motivated to create pride within their school?

Possessing a perception of genuine worth as a result of who you are is an excellent thing. Same goes with possessing confidence in regard to what you do. However, possessing an embellished perception of self-worth could very well be extremely harmful.

C.S. Lewis made available a unique point of view on pride with what I believe was excellent perception. He considered that pride contributes to each and every other depravity. He stated,

"Does this seem to you exaggerated? If so, think it over. I pointed out a moment ago that the more pride one had, the more one disliked pride in others. In fact, if you want to find out how proud you are the easiest way is to ask yourself, 'How much do I dislike it when other people snub me?…'The point is that each person's pride is in competition with everyone else's pride. It is because I wanted to be the big noise at the party that I am so annoyed at someone else being the big noise… Now what you want to get clear is that Pride is essentially competitive, is competitive by its very nature, while the other vices are competitive only, so to speak, by accident.

Pride gets no pleasure out of having something, only out of having more of it than the next man. We say that people are proud of being richer, or cleverer, or better looking than others. If everyone else became equally rich, or clever, or good looking there would be nothing to be proud about. It is the comparison that makes you proud: the pleasure of being above the rest." xxxix

Just how can direct sellers treat other individuals the way they want to be treated if their own engrossment is to defeat them? It is simple, they can't. The truth is if your objective is intended to be richer, wiser, or more appealing as compared to everybody else, your concentration is completely on yourself and your own self-interests.

Over the past two decades, there appears to have been a significant decline in ethics in American society, most notably in business, politics, law, and medicine. Perhaps this is a result of misguided pride?

Pride for a Direct Selling Professional, like anyone else, just isn't a straightforward thing to overcome.

"There is perhaps not one of our natural passions so hard to subdue as pride. Beat it down, stifle it, mortify it as much as one pleases, it is still alive. Even if I could conceive that I had completely overcome it, I should probably be proud of my humility." - Benjamin Franklin

I am in full agreement with Ben Franklin, in that it is next to impossible to fully overcome pride. We should, however, at least make an attempt to overcome it. Pride doesn't only have the possibility to weaken our own ethics; it may also hinder our own overall performance. Pride can easily visually impair you, to your personal defects, along with other men and women's requirements, and also to ethical stumbling blocks that lay across our path.

"When dealing with people, let us remember we are not dealing with creatures of logic. We are dealing with creatures of emotion, creatures bustling with prejudices and motivated by pride and vanity." - Dale Carnegie

Aspect #5 – Priorities

Over the past several years, substantial research has been undertaken into exactly what tends to make businesses extremely prosperous.

"Our research points to one essential element in any successful company. Those that are the best have built a set of core values and lived by them." - Jim Collins

This is also true for the men and women in the Direct Selling Profession. Any time a man or women doesn't understand what his or her priorities need to be he or she can easily discover themselves struggling, simply because he or she is most likely to make very poor decisions.

"Things that matter most must never be at the mercy of things that matter least." – Goethe

I have to acknowledge, this has happened to be an area of some weakness for me personally in the past. When I decided to enter the Direct Selling Profession back in 1985, I didn't fully understand what my priorities should be with a job, starting my own business, a family, friends etc... All I remember back then is that I desired most to be well-liked by people. As a result of this misguided desire, I had a tendency to make poor decisions. I look back on the past 28 years, and my pockets of people-pleasing have led me to fail in a number of significant responsibilities. At times, I would put my new business first in my life, my family would be second, and my job would be a distant third. You can imagine how these priorities could easily impact my career. Over the years, I have moved the pieces of the puzzle around and as I get older, I am much better at setting and maintaining my priorities, but that doesn't mean that the struggle is over. Every single day I still need to control my personal decisions according to these priorities. Remember: its one thing to establish your own values. It's quite another to live them out every single day.

As a Direct Selling Professional, exactly what are your priorities? Precisely what are you currently carrying out now that will still be essential in 50 or 100 years? The material things in life, such as the house you live in, the car you drive, the vacation you took, and the bonus you made won't mean much. As a Direct Selling Professional, precisely what genuinely matters? In the event that you haven't determined your values, I highly encourage you to do so. Then work tirelessly to help keep the insignificant from becoming significant, and the significant from becoming insignificant.

MAINTAINING THE POLISH ON
THE "GOLD STANDARD"

Perhaps it's possible you have realized that greed didn't make the list of aspects that could "discolor" the Golden Rule. That could possibly come as a shock, particularly considering that the main stream media have spoken a great deal about it lately with all the current corporate and business scandals. In the Direct Selling Profession, I am of the belief that, more often than not, it's not necessarily the cash itself that draws men and women across the line ethically. I believe that it's exactly what they could possibly get with it. These direct selling men and women want the power that cash brings, regardless of whether it's power over down line or over circumstances. Perhaps these direct selling men and women just want the pleasure that can be purchased with the cash. Or these direct selling men and women take pride in the actual status of possessions that the cash buys.

If you discover a man or women in the Direct Selling Profession who will give up their integrity for the money, I truly believe you will discover that it is motivated by one of the five aspects previously mentioned.

In the Direct Selling Profession, like everywhere else, men and women are vulnerable to some type of enticement to give up their values. However the encouraging news is that there is a significantly greater fulfillment which comes from not crossing the line. Occasionally you will need to wait for it, nevertheless it will invariably arrive.

OBSERVATIONS FROM
THE RESPONSIBLE DIRECT SELLER™

Let the "*Golden Rule*" be your navigation system. Do not under any circumstances undermine what could be the most valuable part of your life and business.

I have personally witnessed the following:

Up-line putting pressure on their down-line to do something that is in the best interest of their up-line but not the down-line.

Over promising on the opportunity and never delivering on the promises.

Up-line using their success level in the opportunity to strong-arm their down-line.

Up-line making bad and unethical decisions, and then continuing the unethical practice so that no one loses face.

Up-line inserting their priorities into a down-line's life, without taking into consideration the down-line's position.

Etc....

STOP! Everything you do needs to be in the best interest of your down-line! End of story.

CHAPTER 10
CARPE DIEM AND THE "GOLD STANDARD"

I am of the viewpoint that the majority of men and women in the Direct Selling Profession, in their unique approach are searching for a "*golden opportunity.*"

Just out of curiosity, I searched Google for "*golden opportunity*" and in 0.27 seconds it returned 10,200,000 results. If you can image it, there was an offer for it.

Exactly how do you locate a genuine "*golden opportunity*" among all the actual offers which turn out to be, let's say CRAP? The answer lies internally, not externally. The vast majority of Direct Selling Professionals believe their greatest opportunities come from the business opportunity they chose, an investment they were able to make as a result of the money gained from said business opportunity, or some esoteric form. However, the simple truth is that the greatest opportunity you as a Direct Selling Professional have is exactly the same as anyone else; it is to transform exactly who you are. It's similar to giving a position on the Stanley Cup Winning team to a yoga instructor who hasn't trained for their event. The really good news is that the yoga instructor has been given a shot at winning. The not so good news is that the yoga instructor is not prepared for it.

HOW ONE STEP LEADS TO THE NEXT STEP!

It seems apparent that it was a similar kind of challenge for quite a few of the CEOs who ended their careers with a really big bang and demolished their businesses during the past decade. These kinds of "special" men and women had needless to say not carried out the ethical preparation internally prior to attaining power. It ended up being their poor character that persuaded these "people of influence" to make extremely bad decisions, and with just about every bad decision, these men and women got themselves and their companies into much deeper difficulties. Character challenges are similar to a snowball rolling down a hill, once it starts, it get bigger and bigger until finally it reaches the bottom of the hill totally out of control and takes out your neighbor.

It seems that good and evil equally increase in a similar fashion to the way money increases using the power of compound interest. That's the reason why the small choices we make every single day possess such unlimited significance. The tiniest good action performed right now is quite possibly the catalyst for which there's a chance you're capable of going on to wins you have never even dreamed of before. And a lack of action today is something that can come back in the future and bite you in the ass. (Personally, I can attest to this one.)

As a Direct Selling Professional, prior to pursuing any "golden opportunities," start by pursuing the growth and development of powerful character. This will certainly position you extremely well to manage virtually any ethical challenge that could possibly lie in the future and also to take full advantage of your possibilities as soon as your time arrives. Here's how I suggest you proceed:

As A Direct Selling Professional, Every Single Action You Take Is Your Responsibility

This is a concept that is lost on some Direct Selling Professionals. If you happen to be involved, no matter what it is, you are responsible for your actions! Obligation is actually in proportion to the opportunity available to you and me. Do you understand why? Due to the fact any man or women of responsibility can easily trust him or herself to select the right thing above the easy thing.

The definition of "*frustration*" for some Direct Selling Professionals is "*having no one to blame but yourself.*" Rarely do men and women of the Direct Selling Profession who take part in the "blame game" get hold of very many "*golden opportunities.*" And in some cases the very few opportunities these men and women do get hold of fall right through their fingertips. Whenever that takes place, undoubtedly, you will hear the reason why it's not their fault.

There's simply no excuse for falling into any of these categories:

The "Life's Circumstances" Attribution - Direct Selling Professionals who seem to pin the consequence on life's conditions,

The "Woe Is Me" Attribution - Direct Selling Professionals who seem to pin the consequence on previous personal challenges and injuries, and

The "Manure Spreader" Attribution - Direct Selling Professionals who seem to pin the consequence on various other direct sellers for working against them.

In the event that it happens to be your wish to be trusted by other Direct Selling Professionals and you also desire to be successful, you will first need to assume responsibility with regard to your actions. Responsibility here means the actual preparation with regard to opportunity, as well as the cost of success.

As A Direct Selling Professional, Your Personal Discipline Must Be Developed.

Not long ago I read the results of a recent study of more than 400 business executives that reveals that many people who cheat at golf also cheat in business. *"Those who move the ball for a better lie or conveniently forget to count a couple of strokes are also likely to fake reports, juggle accounts, and lie about their business actions. Asked if they cheated at golf, 55% admitted they did…. The challenge now facing America's business executives, as I see it, is not to explain themselves better, but to demonstrate that they take the public's concerns and criticisms seriously. Maybe it's time for Americans to elect Arnold Palmer or Jack Nicklaus President -- someone who understands not only the rules of the game but the importance of playing by them whether he or she is being watched or not. Professional golfers are the only professionals I know who call penalties on themselves for violating the rules of the game. Frankly, I'd like to see that kind of honesty in our nation's leaders and in its business leaders, as well. We need leaders who not only hit the ball straight, but who think straight and talk straight, too."* [xl]

Polls, as any pollster knows, sometimes reveal what men and women think, not necessarily the way they act. Do you know why regardless of whether men and women notice a parallel between games and life, these men and women nonetheless make the decision to take shortcuts? In my opinion the answer lies in their lack discipline. Men and women who neglect to develop personal discipline in many cases are inclined to cheat just to keep up with society. Expertise without having discipline is similar to a baby trying to walk for the very first time. At first, there is abundance of movement, however you can't say for sure if it's destined to be forward, backwards, or back onto their nicely padded bums.

As a Direct Selling Professional, precisely what we choose to do at any given time will in all probability be determined by what we are made of; and just what we are made of is definitely the result of previous years of self-discipline.

Direct Selling Professionals who would like to enhance their character in addition to their likelihood of success need to discipline themselves when it comes to:

Chronology: You can't regulate how much time you are allotted, nevertheless you can manage the way you utilize it.

Drive: It is recommended to always make an effort to make use of your strengths.

Objectives: You can't accomplish everything, which means you need to discipline yourself to carry out the essential things.

Temperament: Unless you master your emotions, they will master you.

Highly effective Direct Selling Professionals, who actually work well with others, thrive on challenges and business opportunities, and don't find discipline to be detrimental or even prohibitive. Over the past 29 years I have had the pleasure of meeting thousands of Direct Selling Professionals, and I can tell you one thing, the ones that are striving to be at the top of their game, love the daily grind and the discipline.

As A Direct Selling Professional, You Need To Realize Your Weaknesses

For almost two and a half decades I had the opportunity to listen to and learn from Dexter & Birdie Yager of Amway fame. Several times a year, in locations across the United States and overseas I would stand stage-side and listen to both Dexter and Birdie speak. Now it's important to understand that they wouldn't come on stage until about 1:00 to 2:00 a.m. and then speak for 3+ hours. And this is during a weekend event that began at 9:00 a.m. and didn't usually end until the wee hours of the morning on Friday and Saturday. This talk that Dexter and Birdie offered was not traditional-style training; it was training about life. A lot of the topics were controversial and I didn't necessarily agree with all that was said, but I loved the dedication to the craft, as well as how they both knew their weaknesses and did something about them.

As a Direct Selling Professional, to know about your weaknesses in advance allows you to prepare yourself and make the necessary changes inside. Men and women who actually recognize their own weaknesses are hardly ever taken by surprise, neither do they permit other individuals to take advantage of their areas of weakness. In distinction, men and women who fool themselves or who pretend that they are strong where they're not just set themselves up to fail.

As A Direct Selling Professional, Your Priorities Need To Line Up Together With Your Values.

Integrity can easily be referred to as making your values as well as your actions fall into line. When a Direct Selling Professional states they believe one thing and then they intentionally take an opposing action, it's apparent that exactly what they lack is integrity. However, what about a Direct Selling Professional who actually doesn't comprehend that his or her steps oppose his or her values? Despite the fact that it's not necessarily purposeful, that man or women still possesses an integrity problem.

So how does a Direct Selling Professional ensure that his or her values and priorities are in alignment?

I think that it is important to understand what integrity really is. The simplest definition of integrity is the state of being whole, entire, or undiminished. Thus, if you happen to be declaring one thing but doing another, you're divided. As a result you have an integrity problem.

"A house divided against itself cannot stand." - Abraham Lincoln

For the Direct Selling Professional, the perfect solution is straightforward, however certainly not simple. What is it?

- Define your values.

- Align your priorities.

As A Direct Selling Professional, Acknowledge Wrongdoing Swiftly and Request Forgiveness

A very important factor which has regrettably characterized the vast majority of the recent much talked about corporate failures happens to be some type of concealment. Senior level executives at Enron, Tyco, and WorldCom etc. all attempted to conceal virtually any wrongdoing. Needless to say, that attitude isn't pervasive simply in business. Men and women of poor character tend to be a lot quicker to conceal compared to admitting wrongdoing.

One of the challenges that I had early on in my direct selling career was the use of an "*optional*" personal development monthly tool package that was offered to the distributors of the network marketing business opportunity I was part of. First of all, I think that it was great that a personal development program existed and was available to the distributors. However, where I felt it crossed the ethical line was that leaders were compensated for their share of the resources that were purchased in their organization. Of course they would promote it, yet in two and a half decades, I never once was recommended any resource not found inside the recommended tool package. In other words the remaining 95 percent that was available.

LET'S COMPARE THE EXAMPLE ABOVE WITH JACK WELCH, CHAIRMAN AND CEO 1981 - 2001, GENERAL ELECTRIC.

Through the 1980s, Welch sought to streamline GE. In 1981 he made a speech in New York City called "Growing fast in a slow-growth economy." Welch worked to eradicate perceived inefficiency by trimming inventories and dismantling the bureaucracy that had almost led him to leave GE in the past. He closed factories, reduced payrolls and cut lackluster old-line units. Welch's public philosophy was that a company should be either No. 1 or No. 2 in a particular industry, or else leave it completely. Welch's strategy was later adopted by other CEOs across corporate America.

Each year, Welch would fire the bottom 10% of his managers. He earned a reputation for brutal candor in his meetings with executives. He rewarded those in the top 20% with bonuses and stock options. He also expanded the broadness of the stock options program at GE from just top executives to nearly one-third of all employees. Welch is also known for destroying the nine-layer management hierarchy and bringing a sense of informality to the company.

During the early 1980s he was dubbed "Neutron Jack" (in reference to the neutron bomb) for eliminating employees while leaving buildings intact. In Jack: Straight From the Gut, Welch states that GE had 411,000 employees at the end of 1980, and 299,000 at the end of 1985. Of the 112,000 who left the payroll, 37,000 were in businesses that GE sold, and 81,000 were reduced in continuing businesses. In return, GE had increased its market capital tremendously. Welch reduced basic research, and closed or sold off businesses that were under-performing.

In 1986, GE acquired RCA. RCA's corporate headquarters were located in Rockefeller Center; Welch subsequently took up an office in the now GE Building at 30 Rockefeller Plaza. The RCA acquisition resulted in GE selling off RCA properties to other companies and keeping NBC as part of the GE portfolio of businesses. During the 1990s, Welch shifted GE business from manufacturing to financial services through numerous acquisitions.

Welch adopted Motorola's Six Sigma quality program in late 1995. In 1980, the year before Welch became CEO, GE recorded revenues of roughly $26.8 billion. By 1999 he was named "Manager of the Century" by Fortune magazine. In 2000, the year before he left, the revenues increased to nearly $130 billion. The company had gone from a market value of $14 billion to one of more than $410 billion at the end of 2004, making it the most valuable company in the world.

Prior to his retirement, there was a lengthy and well-publicized succession planning saga among James McNerney, Robert Nardelli, and Jeffrey Immelt, with Immelt eventually selected to succeed Welch as chairman and CEO. Nardelli became the CEO of Home Depot until his resignation in early 2007, and until recently, was the CEO of Chrysler, while McNerney became CEO of 3M until he left that post to serve in the same capacity at Boeing.

Welch's "walk-away" package from GE was not valued at the time of his retirement, but GMI Ratings estimates its worth at $420 million. [xli]

So what is the comparison between my example above and that of Jack Welch's tenure as Chairman and CEO at General Electric? It lies in the percentage of value added back to the company, the organization and the industry. In my opinion, Jack Welch was worth every dime he was paid and the percentage of value added was off the charts.

As A Direct Selling Professional, Your Finances Require Extra Care

One of the better approaches to accumulate awareness into the character of another Direct Selling Professional man or woman is actually to watch exactly how they manage their money. To gain an even better insight into the topic of managing money, ask the following questions.

Are Direct Selling Professional men and women generous with other people's money but restricted making use of their own?

Do these Direct Selling Professional men and women demand that each and every financial transaction naturally benefit them?

Do these Direct Selling Professional men and women take shortcuts to realize even more wealth?

Precisely what place does money possess in the lives of these Direct Selling Professional men and women?

Cash doesn't transform men and women; it simply reveals what's truly inside them. In the event that a man or woman is normally self-centered or conceited or money grubbing, the cash brings that out for all to see.

Men and women can frequently be tripped up whenever they make amassing greater wealth a greater priority than it ought to be.

I pointed out in the previous chapter that money is certainly nothing more than a tool. However, it is important to point out that it is a very razor-sharp tool; one which if dealt with badly is able to do amazing damage. That's the reason why we as Direct Selling Professionals need to take special care with our finances. In the event that we as Direct Selling Professionals manage the appropriate attitude about money, then it will invariably be a beneficial, valuable tool and not a detrimental one.

If you're concerned about keeping money from becoming the master, try doing the following:

As A Direct Selling Professional, Generate Your Own Personal Income - Men and women who generate what they've got have a much greater regard for the property of other men and women. And with this type of mindset as a Direct Selling Professional you will attempt to receive more bangs for your buck if you have to earn it yourself.

As A Direct Selling Professional, Always Be Meticulously Trustworthy - Bend over backwards to ensure your complete financial transactions are above board, not merely with regard to others, but in addition for yourself.

As A Direct Selling Professional, Become Generous - You often hear that we earn a living by what we generate; however we make a life by what we donate or tithe. Donating or tithing not only assists other individuals as well as liberates all of us; additionally it puts money into the proper perspective much better than anything else you or I can do.

As A Direct Selling Professional, Make Use of Credit Sensibly and Moderately - OK, before you jump all over me and say, "Kevin, how do I do that when just about everything requires a credit card, especially purchases online?" Simple, let's first look back at our goal. Use credit sensibly and moderately. First, only use your credit card when you actually need to. Secondly, be sensible and pay off the balance every 30 days (or prior to your next statement) so that you minimize your accumulation of interest.

As a Direct Selling Professional, actually learning how to have the appropriate attitude with regards to money, as well as how to manage it appropriately (instead of being handled by it) sets the groundwork for several additional character triumphs in a Direct Selling Professional's life.

As A Direct Selling Professional, Place Your Family In Advance Of Your Business.

The variety of job titles and political positions he has attained is actually remarkable: U.S. congressman, ambassador to the United Nations, chief liaison officer in China, head of the CIA, vice president of the United States, and, finally, president of the United States. However when his life in public office concluded, George H.W. Bush declared that he continued to possess the three most significant titles he ever held: husband, father, and grandfather. Without a doubt, that's an awesome perspective on family.

Traditionally, family in the Direct Selling Profession is always promoted from stage as being the second priority behind one's chosen God. However, when you are in the trenches, especially at the beginning of building your business, the expectation is to put everything aside for the next 3 to 5 years and develop your business. Now this may seem contradictory on the surface, but what is really meant by this strategy is to "*always be present.*" So, what does "*always be present*" mean? It simply means that at any given time, you need to take responsibility and focus your 100 percent attention on the task at hand. Example: You're out with your family, so your full attention is on them and not on anything else. You're at your job, your full attention needs to be on your responsibilities, someone is actually compensating you're in good faith that you will. You're working your business; your full attention is on those tasks. It is all about managing your time and blocking out your schedule in an appropriate manner. Is this going to require changes to you and your family? Yes, however the result will be a better use of quality time and your family will become used to the fact that when mom or dad or both are with them they have 100 percent of their attention. Thus, making it easier to get their buy-in for blocking time to build your direct selling business.

As A Direct Selling Professional, Place High Value on Men and Women

Whenever the majority of Direct Selling Professionals take into consideration the development of character, these men and women concentrate on whatever they need to turn out to be, which is excellent, considering that <u>that is the majority of the course of action required.</u>

However in order to make yourself prepared to take hold of the "golden opportunities," you need to do one more thing. As a Direct Selling Professional man or woman you need to value other men and women sufficiently to provide them with a portion of yourself, which is your trust. That, all things considered, is without a doubt the real heart and soul of the Golden Rule.

Years ago I heard this story told from stage by the late George Halsey (the first African American Triple Diamond in Amway history), about how a naval commander by the name of Mike Abrashoff lived the Golden Rule both onboard and on land.

I was always taught that when telling a story from stage, ensure that you attach a point to that story and tie it in.

George began by telling this audience of 50,000+ a bit about Abrashoff's background, so that we got the essence of the man.

Graduated from the U.S. Naval Academy in Annapolis, attained the rank of captain after sixteen years, became military assistant to Dr. William J. Perry when he was Secretary of Defense and then his first command, the USS Benfold where the story of the Golden Rule truly begins.

For the first sixteen years of Mike's career, he went for the gold braid (promotions). He had plenty of success, however for the navy, it wasn't uncommon success. The very last two years Mike decided to go for the

Golden Rule. Mike took command of the USS Benfold as well as he took command of his life. Prior to these two years, Mike had been operating in accordance with what he believed were the Navy's objectives. However, while working for Secretary of Defense Perry, he observed a disengagement from that kind of thought process. When Mike observed his predecessor departing the ship, he thought about what his departure would turn out to be like.

Mike always explained the navy as being very similar to a tree packed with monkeys. In the event that you happen to be at the top of the tree (senior level officer and above), all you ever observe whenever you look down is a bunch of smiling faces looking right back at you. However, if you happen to be a monkey at the bottom of the tree and you look up, your view is best described as "*different*."

Mike made a decision to place himself in the shoes of his sailors. Mike individually and independently interviewed each and every sailor on his ship to determine exactly what each of these sailors valued, after which Mike implemented modifications in response to what the sailors valued, for example sending the ship's cooks to culinary school to become chefs, as well as providing college and University courses on-board his ship. Mike decided to ask his officers to treat the new arriving sailors as they quite simply would want their own children treated (how cool is that). And Mike enabled each and every sailor on board, no matter what rank they held, to generate decisions and make an effort to turn their ship into the best in the Navy, by simply having faith in them and inspiring them with the words: "*It's your ship.*"

Mike quickly noticed that as soon as he started to strive for the Golden Rule, good began to happen on the ship. The moment that Mike started to put men and women instead of a promotion first, the results were positive and exponential. That's exactly what I would refer to as taking advantage of a "*golden opportunity*."

OBSERVATIONS FROM
THE RESPONSIBLE DIRECT SELLER™

If you would like to build a large International Direct Selling Organization, here is how I suggest you proceed:

Take Responsibility for Your Actions - Everything you do or don't do is your responsibility. The faster you adopt this mind-set the faster your organization will grow.

Develop Personal Discipline - You must be able to lead by example. How many direct sellers would you like in your organization with the same personal discipline that you possess today?

Know Your Weaknesses - Know your weaknesses but do not dwell on them. Build your organization to backfill your weaknesses.

Align Your Priorities with Your Values -It all starts with your values. From there your priorities need to be set.

Admit Wrongdoing Quickly and Ask Forgiveness -It's simple. However, it may not be easy. Suck it up and admit your wrongdoing and move on.

Take Extra Care with Finances - Once again, lead by example.

Put Your Family Ahead Of Your Work - This is critical. Why else are you building your business to Financial Freedom unless you want to spend time with your family? You can and should do both. Spend quality time with your family and ensure that they are behind you in your endeavor. Place High Value on People. People are your greatest asset, not you!

CHAPTER 11
THE FOLLOWING STEPS WILL HELP YOU
IMPLEMENT THE "GOLD STANDARD"

Midas Touch Story - The Creative License Edition

In the late 1970's I was attending High School in Calgary, Alberta, Canada. One of the subjects that we were taught but I had very little interest in was Greek Mythology. Even though it was by far my least favorite subject, I did retain the story of King Midas. He had been the king connected with historical Phrygia. On one particular day he was offered the opportunity to assist a friend of his, Dionysus, who just happened to be the god of revelry (which means boisterous festivity), in other words he who have starred on TMZ. Because of this assistance to Dionysus, Midas was awarded a single wish. So being greedy and not fully thinking through his answer and wish request, Midas asked Dionysus to make everything Midas touched turn to gold. Then Poof!!! Midas had the ability to turn anything he touched to gold. Remember, Midas really didn't think this through, even after the first several times that he used his new found talent.

Midas touched a tree, and it turned to gold.

Midas touched a horse, and it became solid gold.

In a matter of minutes, he was becoming the richest man in the world, yet he hadn't figured out how it was going to backfire on himself.

After an afternoon of touching various objects and having them turn to gold, Midas found that he possessed a "*manly*" kind of hunger. So Midas visited his local "*goat-on-a-stick*" stall and ordered a couple of the daily specials. His problems began when his "*daily specials*" also turned to gold, like everything else he touched that afternoon.

So like the great mythical being that he was, he turned to alcohol; in his case, a leather bottle of wine. Anyone want to take a guess at what happened? You guessed it; it turned into the most expensive bottle of wine to date.

However, all of these examples of good luck and hardship hadn't quite percolated to the top of Midas's head because when his daughter snuck up on him during their daily game of "kick the goat," Midas turned around and tagged his daughter and before he could say "you're it," she turned to gold.

Now if you are a parent like me, who has a daughter, a little quiet time would have been nice. But not to ol' Midas, he picked up his "sandal phone" and set an appointment with Dionysus, to have his *new talent* removed.

By nightfall, after he and his daughter waded into the river Pactolus (Manisa Province, Turkey), and washed away all that "*Midas Touch*" ability, he was later seen very happily dancing the night away at a nightclub in downtown Salihli, Turkey.

Pactolus River Trivia - Phrygian river with significant deposits of gold in ancient times. These were attributed to the legendary King Midas, who had been granted the ability to transmute whatever he touched into gold. The king found drawbacks to this power and was permitted to wash it away in the river. Mythological fiction intersects with historical fact in that the Pactolus was source of the wealth of King Croesus, who ruled in the sixth century B.C.E. Both the legendary Midas and historical Croesus survive in figures of speech. One speaks of the "*Midas touch*" and being "*as rich as Croesus*". [xlii]

On a side note, I searched Google for the river and it seems that it is located in the middle of nowhere, between the cities of Ahmetli and Salihli, Turkey. You would have thought with all these gold properties they would have erected some sort of amusement park or something.

THE GENUINE GOLD STANDARD

In today's world, when someone is referred to as having the "*Midas touch*," it's generally intended as a compliment. It's a sign that this particular individual possesses an amazing skill for generating cash. However a single-minded addiction to wealth generation is equally as destructive to a Direct Selling Professional these days as it ended up being during the time of Mr. Midas.

In the profession of Direct Selling, there happen to be an inordinate amount of millionaires and wealthy men and women. If I am not mistaken, our profession has generated more millionaires than any other single profession that exists today.

When we look at these millionaires within the Direct Selling Profession, first of all we need to celebrate them before anything else. The next thing we need to do is compare them to millionaires that were created outside our profession. Ask yourself the following questions:

Are their own desires purely selfish?

Do their preferences run to a grand home, automobiles, fine clothes, a good amount of amusements, and so forth?

Are they any happier, do you think, than you are?

Are they any better morally?

Are they any stronger physically?

Are they better liked by their friends?

There are a few differences between millionaires created within the Direct Selling Profession and those created outside the profession, but none more obvious than the fact that the millionaires in the Direct Selling Profession smile more. Perhaps that is because along with creating a business, they created a lifestyle that included financial freedom and "*time*" freedom.

In this day and age, it is hard not to be selfish at least a little bit. It's an element of human nature. If you're doing so an excessive amount, however, people in your circle of influence could possibly get sick and tired of you. Here is how to stop being selfish:

Try to develop empathy for other people and living creatures. Allow yourself to imagine how they feel, what hurts them or makes them happy. Open your heart.

Look for ways to help; anticipate the needs and feelings of others.

Listen. There is a big difference between hearing something and letting something go in one ear and out the other and actually listening to what people have to say.

Don't interrupt people. Let them finish their sentence, your points can always wait. If it's urgent (like if you have to leave) say "excuse me".

Put the needs of other people before your own. Pay attention to the people in your life to find out what those needs are.

Think about the other person's personality. When choosing gifts or cards, buy something that reflects the personality of the other person. Don't just buy something because it's convenient.

Remember birthdays.

Keep in touch with your friends and relatives.

Volunteer.

Be honest and loyal.

Consider the advice people in your life give you. Take it if it makes sense.

If you have to ask someone for a favor, offer to do something for him or her in return.

Compliment other people. Don't just go on about how great you are.

Make sure to be considerate and include everyone you know and like when inviting people to parties and events. No one likes to be left out.

Don't butt in front of people in line. Also, if you see someone in a walker or a wheelchair, slow down or help them instead of just cutting in front of them.

Be on time. If at all possible, call if you know you are going to be late.

Give your time or kindness to others that need it. Random acts of kindness also make you feel satisfied.

INTRODUCING THE GOLD STANDARD 3.0 LIFE

I am of the belief that you will find there's actual true wealth that happens to be more significant than cash, and it originates from the method in which you connect with other men and women. Men and women who apply the Golden Rule treat other individuals with dignity as well as respect and can be fulfilled knowing that they happen to be living an ethical life.

However, I am here to tell you that it's actually possible to take the Golden Rule to a level above all others, and I call it the *"Gold Standard 3.0!"*

Gold Standard 3.0 is when you establish a *"Midas touch"* with men and women by removing the focus off yourself and precisely what you will gain, and as an alternative, devote 100% of your time to adding value to others.

Giving genuinely is the pinnacle of living. Without question, it helps make our global community a much better place to live. And coincidently in addition it tends to make for much better business. As Direct Selling Professionals, we should certainly possess a much better profession when all members of our profession come to the realization that even though it pays extremely well to invest money in their organization or businesses, as well as, develop their down line (natural resources), the highest dividends are paid when we all invest our money to enhance humanity and develop global *"human resources."* In the event that you desire more than simply a full bank account and you desire to create genuine riches, by truly investing in men and women, then make an effort to live out the following practices:

As A Direct Selling Professional, Treat Men and Women Much Better Than These People Happen To Treat You

We all know that it's an easy task to love the men and women who happen to love us. And deep down within all of us we know that displaying kindness to men and women who happen to treat us well is a bit more than simple common courtesy. However exactly how should we as Direct Selling Professionals react to bad treatment by other men and women? Should we return discourtesy with discourtesy? Should we meet encroachment with encroachment? It doesn't require a sociologist to tell us that it doesn't take much for unkindness to escalate into greater discord. Have a look at a few of these obviously insignificant squabbles that progressed into full blown war:

A disagreement involving the cities of Modena and Bologna, in northern Italy, over a water well bucket about 900 years ago began a war that devastated Europe. (Could have been where the story of the *"pipeline"* that is famous in Direct Selling circles first started?)

A Chinese Emperor on one occasion went to war over the smashing of a teapot. (There are a few "Starbuckites" that fully understand his position)

Sweden and Poland flew at each other's throats in 1654 for the reason that king of Sweden learned that his name in an official dispatch was followed by only two "et cetera's," while the king of Poland had three. (Now I can see Poland doing this but Sweden? Result was IKEA!)

The spilling of a glass of water on the Marque de Torey led to war between France and England. (Enough said)

By throwing a pebble at the Duc de Guise, a small boy caused the massacre of Vassy and the Thirty Years' War. (He obviously missed. I bet he was grounded for that one.)

It requires a Direct Selling Professional of formidable character to treat other individuals better than they treat you. In the event that every Direct Selling Professional practiced the Golden Rule, our global community would be a much better place to be. However take into consideration what type of global community it would be if every Direct Selling Professional endeavored to treat other Direct Selling Professionals much better than they are treated themselves (perhaps adopted that mindset at home).

WELCOME TO THE GOLD STANDARD 3.0!

As A Direct Selling Professional, Walk the Second Mile

What is the second mile and where did that expression come from?

In the 3rd century BC, and for 500 years after, the Roman Empire allowed a Roman officer to force anyone to carry a load one mile. It was the officer's right, and a citizen who declined, did so at his own peril. This first mile was a requirement, however, any length beyond that was a show of respect to the Roman officer. Thus the second mile was born and the expression "*Walk the Second Mile*" began.

So what do I mean when I suggest walking the second mile in the Direct Selling Profession? I am suggesting that you strive to do more than is required. Try and look at the extra mile as being an opportunity to make a positive impact on the lives of other Direct Selling Professionals, and to add value to the men and women in your life.

A Direct Selling Professional that possesses an "*extra-mile*" attitude is a man or woman who:

- Cares more about others than others think is wise.

- Risk more for others than others think is safe.

- Dreams more than others think is practical.

- Expects more than others think is possible.

- Works more than others think is necessary.

"There's no traffic jam on the extra mile." - *Zig Ziglar*

In the event that you as a Direct Selling Professional consistently carry out a lot more than what is anticipated, not only are you going to rise up above the masses, you will assist other individuals to rise up along with you.

Have you at any time sat back and thought that it appeared like lots of people in this world aren't carrying out their own fair share of the work?

The following is a survey that consists of 100 percent irrefutable statistics and proves without a shadow of a doubt that there aren't nearly as many people actually working as you may have thought, and you have absolutely every reason to be tired.

In the United States of America the population is a bit over 315 million.

In the United States, there is a birth every 8 seconds, and death every 12 seconds. [xliii]

106 million people are over 64 years of age and retired. That leaves 209 million of us to do all the work.

People under 20 years of age total 119 million, so that leaves 90 million to do all the work.

There are 34 million who are employed by the government, which leaves 56 million to do the work.

18 million are in the armed forces, which leaves 38 million to do all the work.

Deduct 25 million, the number in state and city offices. That leaves 13 million to do the work.

There are 8 million in hospitals, mental institutions, and various asylums, so that leaves 4 million to do the work.

Now it may interest you to know that there are 3,999,998 people in jails and prisons, so that leaves just 2 people to carry the load.

That's you and me, and I am about ready for a break!

As A Direct Selling Professional, Assist Men and Women Who Can't Help You Back

You and I haven't lived today effectively unless of course we have performed a little something for someone who is unable to ever repay us.

As Direct Selling Professionals we are part of an extremely competitive society. Frequently many of us define our successes by how superior we are to the next individual. And whenever we decide to assist other Direct Selling Professionals, many of us demand that it be a win for us as well. Nevertheless if we as Direct Selling Professionals desire to live a Gold Standard 3.0 life, do something for someone who can never repay you, and do it consistently.

JAMAICA NATIONAL BOBSLED TEAM

The Jamaican national bobsleigh team represented Jamaica in international bobsledding competitions, and first gained fame during their debut in the 1988 Winter Olympic Games in Calgary, Alberta, Canada, where they were seen as underdogs, representing a tropical nation in a winter sport. The team returned to the Winter Olympics again in 1992, 1994, and subsequent competitions. The team failed to qualify for the 2006 and 2010 Winter Olympics.

The team (consisting of Devon Harris, Dudley Stokes, Michael White, and Nelson Stokes) quickly became a fan favorite largely because of their status position as the ultimate 'underdog' story of the games. Not only was there the novelty of having a tropical country compete in a cold-weather sport, but they had very little practice going down a bobsled track before, and they borrowed spare sleds from other countries to compete. In a show of worldly brotherhood, other bobsledders were quick to give them guidance and support. They did not officially finish after losing control of the sled and crashing during one of their four runs. However, they showed significant improvement throughout the games and impressed observers with some fast starts.

This team was the inspiration for a major motion picture, Cool Runnings featuring John Candy as the team's coach. [xliv]

If you want to help people, then embrace the motto of nineteenth century evangelist D. L. Moody, who advised:

Do all you can

To all the people you can

In all the ways you can

For as long as you can

And whenever you can do that for people, who can't do anything for you in return, then you're really developing your Gold Standard 3.0, because you are adding value to the lives of others.

Need an inspiration regarding helping people? Take a look here:

- Donate your time to a local charity

- Do what you do best for someone for free

- Foster a homeless animal

- Volunteer at your local school

- Volunteer for a local non-profit whose work is one of your passions

- Take your pet to an assisted living center to visit

- Inspire Others

- Pick a cause and lobby for it

- Bake a cake for your neighbor

- Pay for a toll

- Donate money and time

- Organize your co-workers to take on a cause

- Send an e-mail about how people can make a difference

- Give up one Saturday to do something to help

- Make a difference in your community

- Fundraise for a needy family

- Scrapbook for a "Make-A-Wish" child

- Donate meals to a needy family

- Learn about a charity in need and inform others

- Become a Big Brother or Sister

- Invite a less fortunate child to participate in activities with your family

- Collect toys for children in foster care

- Teach someone to read

- See a need? Fill it

As A Direct Selling Professional, Carry Out Things That Are Right when it's Natural to Do the Wrong Things

Probably my favorite example of someone carrying out a task when it would have been natural to do the wrong thing is the story of Cynthia Cooper and her role as whistle-blower, resulting in the downfall of WorldCom.

So who is Cynthia Cooper you say? Well she is not a politician and has never run for public office. And yet without her efforts, the Sarbanes-Oxley Act - the most sweeping investor-protection legislation passed by Congress since the Great Depression - might never have been enacted.

In early 2002, following the collapse of Enron, angry lawmakers held hearings, threatened auditors and warned CEOs that sleight-of-hand accounting tricks would not be tolerated. The Justice Department even indicted one auditing firm, Arthur Andersen, essentially putting it out of business.

But by June of 2002, the sound and fury surrounding Enron's collapse had subsided. Congress planned to pass some form of legislation, but the passions that swayed lawmakers in the winter of 2002 had eased. Business as usual was coming back into fashion.

Then WorldCom dropped a bombshell: It disclosed a $3.8 billion accounting fraud of its own, sowing panic among investors. The company filed for bankruptcy protection, wiping out its shareholders, and the public demanded immediate action. Congress complied, passing the law known as the Sarbanes-Oxley Act.

But the only reason WorldCom's board of directors discovered the accounting fraud was through the efforts of the company's internal auditor, Cynthia Cooper, and her dedicated subordinates.

Cynthia Cooper's adventures at WorldCom come to life in her personal account. The Mississippi native describes how, early in 2002, at the request of a colleague, she began investigating some unusual accounting entries over at WorldCom's wireless division. Little did she know at the time, but Cooper had picked up a thread that would eventually lead to WorldCom's accounting manipulations.

She approaches a partner at WorldCom's auditing firm, Arthur Andersen, to discuss the matter further. The Andersen partner assures her that any aggressive accounting entries in wireless are balanced out on a corporation wide basis.

The next day, Cooper leaves work early to squeeze in an appointment at the hairdresser. With an 8-month-old daughter at home, it's a rare opportunity for some quiet time. But while she's in the middle of the bleaching process, shrouded in tin foil, with hairdryers blaring all around, she gets a call saying that Scott Sullivan, WorldCom's boy-wonder chief financial officer, wants to speak to her immediately.

She phones in to the office, and Sullivan chides her for snooping around the wireless accounting treatments. He tells her not to discuss the matter with Andersen auditors, but to channel all her queries through his own deputy, David Myers.

It's like a scene from a Lifetime "*Moment of Truth*" movie. Cooper has no idea that Sullivan is hiding a massive fraud that will result in the biggest bankruptcy in U.S. history, sending him and his boss to jail, but her gut instinct tells her that something is amiss.

"No one wants to believe their boss is perpetrating a fraud, you want to believe there is a valid explanation." Cynthia Cooper

After several months, Cooper's team figures out that Sullivan's department has made $3.8 billion in questionable accounting entries that had the effect of inflating WorldCom's earnings.

Sullivan, the CFO, ultimately pleaded guilty to several crimes and testified on behalf of the government against WorldCom CEO Bernie Ebbers. Ebbers was convicted and sentenced to 25 years in prison. Sullivan, because of his cooperation, got five years. [xlv]

As A Direct Selling Professional, Keep Your Promises Even If It Hurts Like Hell

Have you ever made a promise to your child and then were not able to keep that promise? In my opinion that is among the worst things you could ever do to your child.

In late 2009 I began to feel significant pain if I happened to sit too long (no problem, I sit at my computer every day for 10 to twelve hours :)). A few months later, in January 2010 I meet with my General Physician and begin a long and painful investigation into the source of this pain.

By April of 2010 after seeing an Urologist and General Surgeon, we started the imaging process. However, by May 2010 without answers, the pain becoming unbearable, and two emergency visits in as many weekends, I was finally admitted to hospital.

I will spare you the gory details (they are quite spectacular and have the ability to completely shut down a conversation), and only say that in 2010 I had one surgery and 2011 I had two. During both 2010 and 2011 I spent the vast majority of my time in bed and on a significant dose of painkillers, unable to work.

As 2012 began and the pain lessened slightly, I began to move around a bit more and attempted to work, but found it difficult with the pain limit and pain killer dosage. In September, I began to feel what I can best describe as a pain within a pain. In February 2013 on a routine visit to my surgeon, we discovered that the problem had returned and that I would require an additional surgery.

During this time I had fully removed myself from making commitments to social functions or family outings. My modus operandi was that I would have to wait to see how I felt at the time of departure. I sure you can guess that 98% of the time, I stayed home in bed.

In March 2013, I made a stupid mistake and promised my daughter (7 years old) that I would attend her gymnastics competition. Big mistake!

I was not able to attend; however, I was able to put her to bed that evening. As I lay with her, her head on my shoulder I listened to her tell me all about her competition. I could hear her try to hold back the sobs, but the tears seemed to burn as they dampened my shirt.

That was my "*literal*" lesson on Keeping Your Promises Even If It Hurts like Hell.

THE GOLD STANDARD

As a Direct Selling Professional, exactly where are you presently centering your attention? Are you actually attempting to build a **Gold Standard 3.0** life? Exactly what opportunities are you presently going after? In the event that you were able to seize them, just what rewards are they going to bring? Would they bring wealth? How about a promotion? Would they bring recognition? Will your walls be filled with awards? Let's put them in perspective. Take this quiz:

Name the five wealthiest people in the world.

Name the last five Heisman Trophy winners.

Name the last five winners of the Miss America contest.

Name ten direct sellers who have won the Nobel Prize.

Name the last half-dozen Academy Award winners for best actor and actress.

Name the last decade's World Series winners.

So, just how well did you do? Exactly how many names did you actually know? 75%? 50%? 25%? These men and women and their teams, the very best in the world at what they do, have accomplished a considerable amount. These men and women have demonstrated that they possess the special touch in their specialization, and as a result they have accomplished an amazing amount of personal recognition. However, exactly what type of influence do they have? More specifically, exactly how much influence have they had on you? (Obviously not much if you can`t even remember most of their names.)

Now, I want you to take another quiz:

- Name three teachers who inspired you to achieve in school.

- Name three friends who helped you through a difficult time.

- Name five direct sellers who taught you something worthwhile.

- Name three direct sellers who made you feel appreciated and special.

- Name five direct sellers with whom you enjoy spending time.

- Name half a dozen heroes whose stories have inspired you.

Perhaps you may very well not have scored 100 % on the 2nd quiz either, however I'm confident that your score ended up being much better than on the very first one. Why am I confident? Simply because these would have been the men and women who had the golden touch in your own life. Adding value to you appeared to be extremely important to them. These men and women focused on other individuals, not merely getting ahead financially. In the event that you wish to do something which is likely to make an impact over and above your own life, then treat men and women much better than they treat you, walk the extra mile, help people who cannot help you, do right when it's natural to do wrong, and keep your promises even when it hurts.

Kevin D. McNabb

OBSERVATIONS FROM
THE RESPONSIBLE DIRECT SELLER™

It starts today with a decision. Remember, from this point forward, you are responsible for your actions and inactions.

Making Sure It's Real - Remember, everything you decide in your business has either a positive or negative impact on more than just you. In Direct selling there is no room for selfish thinking.

How Not To Be Fooled - Start looking for ways to give to others. This will keep you focused on other direct sellers and not yourself.

As a Direct Selling Professional, you need to treat people better than they treat you. This may sound odd, but giving back more than you would expect will come back to you in exponential ways.

As a Direct Selling Professional, be prepared to walk the second mile. If you are not willing to walk the extra mile, do not expect others to do the same. This obviously has to do with your down-line. Do not expect them to do what you do. Remember: they will do 50% of what you do right and 100% of what you do wrong. As a Direct Selling Professional, be prepared to help people who can't help you.

Helping people is not about getting something back in return. It is about doing the right thing. Start looking for ways to help others that do not benefit you. You will be surprised how it positively affects your business and your life.

As a Direct Selling Professional, do right when it's natural to do wrong. If it is natural to do the wrong thing, watch out, it will come back to bite you! And guess what, you won't even know where it came from!

Do the right thing 100% of the time. Think of it this way: what percentage of faithful would you like your spouse to be in your relationship?

As a Direct Selling Professional, always keep your promise even when it hurts. Sometimes we make a promise that, if kept, will have a negative financial impact. Keep it anyway. Not only is it the right thing to do, but you will be amazed at the goodwill it will produce. If you are trying to build an international business, stop thinking small picture and adopt big picture thinking!

CHAPTER 12
CONCLUSION: PURSUE THE GOLD STANDARD 3.0 LIFE

In wrapping up this book, I want to conclude by simply asking you as a Direct Selling Professional, two final questions.

1. As a Direct Selling Professional, exactly what would you wish to accomplish?

a. Precisely what goals have you established for you and your family?

b. Exactly where do you wish your small business to take you?

c. Just what impact on your own community or the global community do you desire to make?

It's extremely helpful to take into consideration these kinds of factors mainly because it really helps to establish the particular path for your life.

2. As a Direct Selling Professional, exactly how do you plan to accomplish it?

That's essential mainly because it establishes the mood pertaining to exactly how you will live your life, as well as, influences precisely how you are going to turn out.

I have faith that there are a couple of fundamental paths to achievement a Direct Selling Professional has the opportunity to choose. First, you may opt to go for the gold. Second, you can pursue a **Gold Standard 3.0** life that is supercharged by the Golden Rule.

In our world, there have been countless men and women out there who have pursued the gold and who appear on the surface to have accomplished pretty much all life has to offer. However, appearances can often be misleading.

1923 EDGEWATER BEACH HOTEL, CHICAGO - THE NINE FINANCIERS, A PARABLE ABOUT POWER

Legend has it that in 1923, a meeting of America's most powerful men took place at the Edgewater Beach Hotel in Chicago. Attending the meeting were the following nine financiers and power brokers:

- the president of America's largest steel company,

- the president of America's largest utility company,

- the president of America's largest gas company,

- the president of the New York Stock Exchange,

- the president of the Bank of International Settlements,

- the nation's greatest wheat speculator,

- the nation's greatest bear and speculator on Wall Street,

- the head of the world's greatest monopoly,

- A member of President Harding's cabinet.

It was said to have been both a celebration of their success as well as an opportunity to plan their future exploits and dominance. These were the captains of their respective industries and some of the most successful businessmen of the era.

But how did things turn out for these distinguished gentlemen?

Within 25 years, all of these great men had met a horrific end to their careers or their lives:

The president of the largest steel company, Charles Schwab, died a bankrupt man; the president of the largest utility company, Samuel Insull, died penniless; the president of the largest gas company, Howard Hobson, suffered a mental breakdown, ending up in an insane asylum; the president of the New York Stock Exchange, Richard Whitney, had just been released from prison; the bank president, Leon Fraser, had taken his own life; the wheat speculator, Arthur Cutten, died penniless; the head of the world's greatest monopoly, Ivar Krueger the "*match king*", also had taken his life; and the member of President Harding's cabinet, Albert Fall, had just been given a pardon from prison so that he could die at home.

And as for the Wall Street Bear, Jesse Lauriston Livermore, famous speculator in the stock and commodities markets, his end is perhaps the most tragic of all. A week after Thanksgiving in 1940, Jesse walked into the Sherry-Netherland Hotel in New York, had two drinks at the bar while scribbling something in his notebook, then proceeded to the cloak room where he sat on a stool and shot himself in the head. He was 62 and left behind $5 million, down from the $100 million fortune he had amassed just ten years earlier. [xlvi]

And the note he had scribbled?

"My dear Nina: Can't help it. Things have been bad with me. I am tired of fighting. I can't carry on any longer. This is the only way out. I am unworthy of your love. I am a failure. I am truly sorry, but this is the only way out for me. Love Laurie"

There are three major lessons we can take from this parable:

Those who are on top now are not certain to finish in that position and are not guaranteed everlasting success or happiness.

Be careful whom you choose to idolize.

The life of a professional speculator is an unpleasant one, filled with highs and lows but ultimately unsatisfying and, in all probability, mentally ruinous. Look no further than the example of history's greatest speculator for proof of this.

Frequently Direct Selling Professional men and women, who pursue the gold, swap just about everything else of significance in their lives for the chance to hold the gold ring. However the majority of those eventually lose those material gains. Even though temporary success may come to numerous men and women who position the acquisition of wealth first, you are able to idly evaluate the quality of their lives by taking a look at their later years. After that it becomes much easier to see if they're a Jack Welch, Chairman & CEO, GE or Mike Abrashoff, Commander of the USS Benfold, or perhaps they are really much more like Jeffrey Skilling, CEO of Enron or Bernard Ebbers, CEO of WorldCom.

There's an enormous amount of distinction between men and women who choose to pursue the gold and people who pursue the Gold Standard 3.0 life that is supercharged with the Golden Rule:

Direct Selling Professionals Who Only Pursue the Gold	Direct Selling Professionals Who "*Choose*" to Pursue the Gold Standard 3.0 Life
Ask, "*What can you do for me?*"	Ask, "*What can I do for you?*"
Make convenient decisions.	Make character decisions.
Sacrifice family for finances.	Sacrifice finances for family.
Develop a rationale for their actions.	Develop relationships with their actions.
Possess a "*me-first*" mindset.	Possess "*another first*" mindset.
Count their dollars.	Count their friends.
Base their values on their worth.	Base their worth on their values.

MARY KAY ASH - A PIONEER

Best known For - Entrepreneur Mary Kay, founder of Mary Kay Inc., built a profitable business from scratch that created new opportunities for women to achieve financial success.

Synopsis

Born May 12, 1918, in Hot Wells, Texas, Mary Kay Ash left the traditional workplace after watching yet another man whom she had trained get promoted over her. She started her own cosmetics company, using incentive programs and other strategies to give her employees the chance to benefit from their achievements. Mary Kay's marketing skills and people savvy soon led her company to enormous success.

Early Career

Business leader and entrepreneur Mary Kay Ash was born Mary Kathlyn Wagner on May 12, 1918, in Hot Wells, Texas. Ash was a pioneer for women in business, building a substantial cosmetics empire. In 1939, Ash became as a salesperson for Stanley Home Products, hosting parties to encourage people to buy household items. She was so good at making the sale that she was hired away by another company, World Gifts, in 1952. Ash spent a little more than a decade at the company, but she quit in protest after watching yet another man that she had trained get promoted above her and earn a much higher salary than hers.

Entrepreneurial Venture

After her bad experiences in the traditional workplace, Ash set out to create her own business at the age of 45. She started with an initial investment of $5,000 in 1963. She purchased the formulas for skin lotions from the family of a tanner who created the products while he worked on hides. With her son, Richard Rogers, she opened a small store in Dallas and had nine salespeople working for her. Today there are more than 1.6 million salespeople working for Mary Kay Inc. around the world.

The company turned a profit in its first year and sold close to $1 million in products by the end of its second year driven by Ash's business acumen and philosophy. The basic premise was much like the products she sold earlier in her career. Her cosmetics were sold through at-home parties and other events. But Ash strove to make her business different by employing incentive programs and not having sales territories for her representatives. She believed in the golden rule - treat others as you want to be treated - and operated by the motto: *God first, family second and career third.*

Ash wanted everyone in the organization to have the opportunity to benefit from their successes. Sales representatives - Ash called them consultants - bought the products from May Kay at wholesale prices and then sold them at retail price to their customers. They could also earn commissions from new consultants that they had recruited.

MARY KAY
COSMETICS

Commercial Success

All of her marketing skills and people savvy helped make Mary Kay Cosmetics a very lucrative business. The company went public in 1968, but it was bought back by Ash and her family in 1985 when the stock price took a hit. The business itself remained successful and now annual sales exceed $2.2 billion, according to the company's website.

At the heart of this profitable organization was Ash's enthusiastic personality. She was known for her love of the color pink and it could be found everywhere, from the product packaging to the Cadillac's she gave away to top-earning consultants each year.

She seemed to sincerely value her consultants, and once said "*People are a company's greatest asset.*"

Her approach to business attracted a lot of interest. She was admired for her strategies and the results they achieved. She wrote several books about her experiences, including Mary Kay: The Success Story of America's Most Dynamic Businesswoman (1981), Mary Kay on People Management (1984) and Mary Kay: You Can Have It All (1995).

Personal Life

While she stepped down from her position as CEO of the company in 1987, Ash remained an active part of the business. She established the Mary Kay Charitable Foundation in 1996. The foundation supports cancer research and efforts to end domestic violence. In 2000, she was named the most outstanding woman in business in the 20th century by Lifetime Television.

The cosmetics mogul died on November 22, 2001, in Dallas, Texas. By this time, the company she created had become a worldwide enterprise with representatives in more than 30 markets. She will be best remembered for building a profitable business from scratch that created new opportunities for women to achieve financial success.

Married three times, Ash had three children - Richard, Ben and Marylyn - by her first husband J. Ben Rogers. The two divorced after Rogers returned from serving in World War II. Her second marriage to a chemist was brief; he died of a heart attack in 1963, just one month after the two married. She married her third husband, Mel Ash, in 1966, and the couple stayed together until Mel's death in 1980. [xlvii]

That's the beauty of living in accordance with a **Gold Standard 3.0** life that is supercharged by the Golden Rule. The simple truth is, if men and women who pursue the gold get very fortunate, they acquire some gold. However those men and women, who pursue the **Gold Standard 3.0** life, not merely have the opportunity to accomplish economic wealth, but additionally to obtain other rewards that cash simply can't offer. Men and women, who live by the **Gold Standard 3.0** life, provide themselves an opportunity to have it all!

OBSERVATIONS FROM
THE RESPONSIBLE DIRECT SELLER™

Whether you decide to build a small business or a large international business, you get to decide whether or not it will be run in an ethical way.

Make a decision today to run your life and your business using the Golden Rule and forget just going after the money.

There are so many more important things than just money. Don't find out the hard way what they really are.

We get very few opportunities to see our life's destiny.

Make your family number one and your business number two.

Treat everyone better than you would like to be treated and ensure that the people that you do business with feel valued, appreciated, trusted, respected, understood, and never taken advantage of.

We have a volunteer army! Our biggest asset is people! Don't ever forget it!

CHAPTER 13
SPECIAL THANKS TO A FEW KEY
ORGANIZATIONS
AND WHAT'S NEXT FOR THE AUTHOR

The profession of direct selling is complex in nature; its foundation is diversity and has a global reach.

There are a number of organizations out there fighting the "*good*" fight; however, I would like to take this opportunity to specially acknowledge five of them.

1. Keeper Catran-Whitney, Founder Nexus Worldwide Media Group, LLC (KeeperCatranWhitney.com, Direct Selling Live, MLM Black Woman, Distributor Magazine, Direct Selling Live 360° Global, 100MillionVoicesProject.com)

2. Nicki Keohohou, CEO and Co-founder & Grace Keohohou, President and Co-founder, Direct Selling Women's Alliance

3. The CEO Council and Board of Directors for the World Federation of Direct Selling Associations

4. Board of Directors, the Direct Selling Association (USA)

5. Board of Directors, the Direct Sellers Association (Canada)

WHAT'S NEXT FOR THE AUTHOR?

First thing on my agenda is to continue to build The Responsible Direct Seller Series ™ (http://theresponsibledirectsellerseries.com/) into the #1 Site on the Internet for Personal Growth and Development that has been designed specifically for the Direct Selling profession.

Second is to continue to write books. In late 2006, while on vacation in Charleston, South Carolina I outlined a total of 60 books that I would like to write and publish over the next 10 years.

Thirdly, I want to personally address a need in the direct selling profession for an association that represents the individual distributor and not just the companies within the profession.

I have long been concerned that the individual distributor is not effectively represented on the global stage.

The time is right to create a global distributor association that "*fully*" represents all aspects for the direct selling distributor.

Many have tried a version of this in the past, and whether it was the timing or the wrong people, it did not work out. Well, I truly believe the timing is right, and I know how to put together the right team.

Direct selling is the selling connected with a consumer product or service, person-to-person, fully removed from a fixed retail store location, promoted by means of independent sales representatives that happen to be characteristically also referenced to as consultants, distributors or other titles. Direct sellers are definitely not employees of any direct selling company.

These distributors are involved in such similar and diverse marketing channels as MLM, Network Marketing, Party Plan and person-to-person sales.

In the past, these marketing channels have been separated because it was felt that they were in no way similar in their business development methods. In my opinion, this is not even close to being true.

Sure, specific techniques and strategies may be distinct to a particular marketing channel, but a substantial amount of individual development (leadership, personal development, etc...) transcends the market channels.

Now, I am not going to get into specifics, but suffice it to say, this global distributor association will be all encompassing, technologically advanced and will meet the needs of today's distributors. I am excited and I look forward to the challenge.

Keep your eyes open for the next chapter in this story.

Do something great with your life... Today!

CHAPTER 14
KEEPER CATRAN-WHITNEY
"THE AMBASSADOR OF HOPE"

The Man

We quite often hear in the Direct Selling Profession about making a positive change in people's lives, helping others achieve financial freedom as well as the amount of good one is capable of doing with the financial rewards received from an unlimited income. Nevertheless, I believe that our profession in general should take a step back to the day when we all first considered the opportunity of direct selling. Exactly what emotions were running through our hearts? Precisely, what emotions are running through the hearts of the new prospective recruit? That brand new prospective recruit is merely experiencing, "the feeling that what is wanted can be had or that events will turn out for the best," in other words they are experiencing "hope." What exactly are we doing as a profession to understand that feeling and encourage that emotion? Well, a man whom I am honored to call my friend is leading the charge in this area and I can't personally imagine a better person than Keeper to be our profession's *"Ambassador of Hope."*

This man is intelligent and extremely dynamic, who understands exactly what hope is all about, mainly because it was hope that got him through the darkest moments of his life.

Keeper, the founder of Nexus Worldwide Media Group, LLC grew up in South Central Los Angeles with four sisters and three brothers and experienced suffering in his life that the majority of us can scarcely imagine. His family was dirt poor and had to fight the rats and the roaches for their daily food. When they weren't homeless, Keeper attended nine different grade schools and experienced the emotional roller coaster of being impacted by one negative step-father after another. Then Keeper experienced his biological father who was a drug addict and alcoholic die of an overdose. Keeper was able to overcome these setbacks and was accepted into college, where unfortunately he was forced to quit helping feed his family of ten.

So what helped Keeper overcome these seemingly insurmountable obstacles? HOPE!

Throughout all those disheartening experiences, Keeper maintained the feeling that what he wanted could be had and that no matter what he chose to do would turn out for the best.

Keeper is an energetic communicator who draws on his life's experiences to get his message across, which is remarkable considering he is afflicted with severe stuttering.

Armed with his hope and life experiences, Keeper has built a solid communication empire that benefits the Direct Selling Profession in ways that most people are now only understanding.

He is a survivor, a powerful communicator, a wonderful and dedicated family man and someone I call a friend.

www.KEEPERCATRANWHITNEY.com

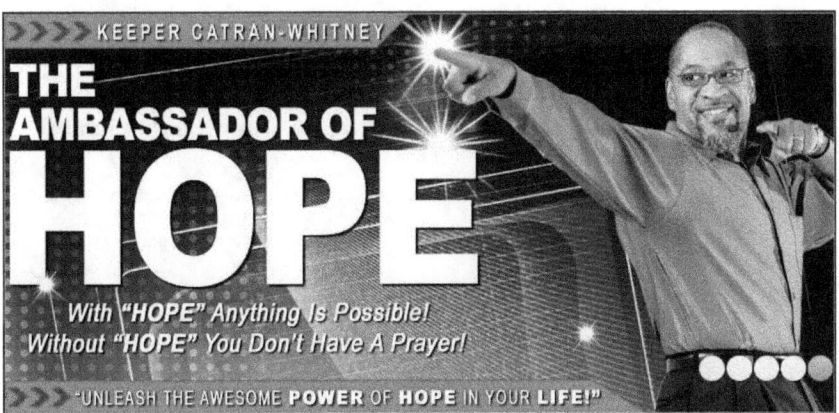

Keeper has spent so much time over the past several years creating multi-media, communication platforms for the benefit of the Direct Selling Profession, that it is now time for him to step out and share his experiences through dynamic speaking engagements. Visit Keeper and learn more about *The Ambassador of Hope.*

DIRECT SELLING LIVE – (www.DIRECTSELLINGLIVE.COM/)

Direct Selling Live is the Direct Selling Professions online television network. This multi-media experience provides direct sellers access to such amazing programming as:

- **The Power 50 Channel** - Direct selling and network marketing's 50 most powerful, most influential people worldwide.

  The Business Files - Direct Selling's source for Innovative & Creative News, Journalism & Original Content.

- **Industry Live Events** – Access to Direct Selling Live Events around the world.

- **On the Air with Keeper** - is direct selling's first ever internet news, information and entertainment TV show that looks at news and events inside and outside of direct selling that shapes our vast global community. **The Recruit** - A Direct Selling Reality Show

- **The POWER 30 List**

- Gays & Lesbians in Direct Selling

- And so much more...

MLM BLACK WOMAN
(www.MLMBLACKWOMAN.NING.COM/)

Direct Selling's Global Voice For People of Color & Diversity
MLMBlackWOMAN
Knowledge, Equality, Tolerance and Progress   A division of NeXus

Direct Selling's global voice for people of color and diversity. The largest diversity community of people of color in direct selling!

Recently, Keeper was contacted by the original founder, British Hill (TV Host, On Air Personality, TV Host Trainer and Coach) to take over MLMBlackWoman.com because of career time restrictions.

Like everything Keeper does, he stepped in and is in the midst of adding his experience and a whole new direction to MLMBlackWoman.com

DIRECT SELLING LIVE 360° GLOBAL
(www.DSL360GLOBAL.COM/)

This is an exciting time for DSL360Global; it is undergoing a complete directional change and is poised to make history. The future for DSL360Global is to become the very first direct selling think tank that will tackle business, social and political issues that directly impact the profession.

In 2012 a significant increase in politics by direct selling company owners prompted Keeper to want to establish DSL360Global as a direct selling think tank to add a voice to the more than 16 million distributors in the United States. With the owners of direct selling companies looking after their own interests without any regard for the individual distributor, it is time for someone to speak on behalf of the distributor when it comes to political decisions and policy debates. With the strength of the distributor base, perhaps politicians will take notice of the more than 16 million voters.

100MILLIONVOICESPROJECT.COM

Direct Selling has been in existence for well over 150 years and during this time, it is safe to say that it has impacted the lives over well over 100 million people worldwide.

The idea behind this project is to collect the stories that make up the history of the Direct Selling Profession.

CHAPTER 15
NICKI AND GRACE KEOHOHOU
DIRECT SELLING WOMEN'S ALLIANCE

The Direct Selling Women's Alliance started around an average small kitchen table when a group of women shared a vision of providing an opportunity for other individuals to live their lives more completely, while at the same time

balancing their personal and professional needs. Never, in the 100 + year history of the Direct Selling Profession, has there been an association dedicated to serving independent Direct Selling Professionals, such as network marketers and party plan professionals. Small business owners and entrepreneurs from around the globe now have a place to call their own... an alliance developed with their success under consideration; an alliance to support the Direct Selling Profession.

MEET THE DSWA CO-FOUNDERS

Meet Nicki and Grace, the founders of the Direct Selling Women's Alliance.

Both of these women share a vision and determination and have dedicated their professional lives to the enhancement of the profession through the establishment of an Alliance which is exclusively dedicated to serving the needs of independent direct sellers around the world.

NICKI KEOHOHOU, CEO AND CO-FOUNDER, WABC CERTIFIED BUSINESS COACH

Nicki started her career as a teacher and coach, which naturally led her to a career in direct selling that has spanned more than 35 years.

Having built successful organizations from the ground up, Nicki's expertise as a leading distributor assisted her to develop a deep love for the profession as well as an enthusiastic knowledge of the difficulties and pleasures of building a flourishing organization.

With her heart focused on adding further value to the profession, Nicki joined the corporate field, serving on the executive teams of top direct selling companies throughout the world.

This subsequently lead her to create her very own consulting & training company through which she has trained thousands of direct sellers worldwide.

Nicki's passion for start-ups motivated her to provide consulting and writing services for numerous companies and organizations within the profession. She brings expertise in the areas of concept development, implementation, marketing and operations, all of which she now brings to the DSWA. Her passion is in education and leadership development.

She received a Bachelor of Arts degree in Business Administration and Education, and her teacher's certification from Central Washington University. She is also a graduate of the University of Illinois Chicago Network Marketing Certification Program and is a certified business coach with the Worldwide Association of Business Coaches.

Nicki was recently named as one of the top 25 Female Executives in the State of Hawaii and was listed as one of the top 30 Female Entrepreneurs in America.

When Nicki is not traveling with speaking and consulting engagements she lives in beautiful Hawaii with her husband, Saffery, of almost 40 years. Her greatest joys are serving others and investing time with her children and grandchildren.

GRACE KEOHOHOU, PRESIDENT AND CO-FOUNDER, WABC CERTIFIED BUSINESS COACH

Since elementary school, Grace continues to be actively involved in direct selling. As a young girl, she attended in-home shows, conventions and tradeshows with her Mother, DSWA Co-founder Nicki Keohohou. Today, she is a seasoned entrepreneur dedicated to the people of the Direct Selling Profession.

Now she is reaching direct sellers in more than 29 countries through her speaking, writing and the DSWA's educational programs. Grace is a Co-Author of the DSWA's Best Selling Book Build It Big - 101 Insider Secrets from Top Direct Selling Experts, More Build It Big, and Mom Entrepreneur.

She is a certified coach with the DSWA's Coach Excellence School, the only coaching school in the world having a focus on the Direct Selling Profession and credentialed through the WABC (Worldwide Association of Business Coaches).

Grace recently received, on behalf of the DSWA, the honor of being named the National Advocate of the Year for Working Mothers. She was also named the 4th Most Influential Woman in the 2009 International Direct Selling Profession.

One of Grace's philanthropic passions is Kids 4 Kids, a Hawaii based community program that she founded along with her children that was designed to provide school supplies for children in need. Grace's greatest joy is supporting and encouraging people to achieve their dreams and life's purpose. She loves living in Hawaii and sharing her time with family and friends.

DSWA FOR PROFESSIONAL ENTREPRENEURS

Our goal is simple—to encourage Direct Selling Professionals to see themselves as capable of being anything they want and fulfill their unique purpose. Direct selling entrepreneurs deserve to feel and act with all their power, and the DSWA is designed to equip and inspire them to do just that. The DSWA understands what it is like to lead with your heart while steering with your mind. We bring the best of both worlds together as a way of allowing independent business owners to be fully engaged in all aspects of their life.

The DSWA is a community of like-minded professionals who value the independence of having their own business. We support them every step of the way through our resource rich website and leading edge virtual training courses relevant to the Direct Selling Profession. We enrich the profession by providing personal and professional training through collaborative leadership retreats and an annual convention called "Celebration," with attendees representing hundreds of companies. The DSWA also offer extensive benefits geared toward making life easier: options for health care, discounts on office supplies and rental cars, free e-books and much more.

Bringing a message of integrity and hope to a local level, the DSWA Chapter program connects women and creates grassroots communities. These Chapter meetings educate and uplift, fulfilling the needs of local sellers across the globe. Whether a novice or a top leader, all members are valued and acknowledged for whom they are. As an open and safe forum for sharing and growing, Chapter meetings allow attendees to learn powerful lessons from each other.

DIRECT SALES, PARTY PLAN, NETWORK MARKETING MOTIVATION

Direct selling, which includes party plan, network marketing and person-to-person sales, offers options to those recently unemployed or those whose jobs may be in jeopardy. Sometimes, just a few hundred dollars a month can mean the difference between keeping your home and losing it to foreclosure. It's also liberating to know that in this profession, glass ceilings are no longer hit, they are shattered! We've seen repeatedly that direct selling can survive any economy. As a matter of fact, this profession thrives in tough economies because people are looking for quality products at a good price delivered to their door. That extra bit of knowledge, motivation, and opportunity provided by the DSWA makes all the difference.

We are excited to say that what began over a kitchen table discussion in a little condo has grown into an international association boasting members from the U.S., Canada, Spain, the United Kingdom, Australia, New Zealand, and beyond. The processional effect of touching women's lives has overflowed into direct selling companies, across gender and into the next generation.

One example of this phenomenal momentum is our Build it Big and More Build it Big books. Almost like a Cinderella story, DSWA was approached by a publisher to create its own series of books. Because of the reach of the DSWA, top performers from across the profession engaged in sharing their best and brightest ideas in order to empower others to success and each book has reached the #1 position on multiple best seller lists.

We have also seen growth within families. Children raised in direct selling homes follow in their parents' footsteps by starting their own businesses and, in at least one case, purchased their first home before turning twenty-one. Another excellent example of the direct selling opportunity is the high success rate of recent immigrants from diverse cultures taking advantage of the American dream!

The DSWA honors and respects the differences in people and recently created the DSWA Diversity Center to better serve all Direct Selling Professionals. In essence, a new sales community has sprung into existence that is based on the principles that bind us together: Service, Trust, Authenticity, Integrity and Respect.

The DSWA Global Foundation offers scholarships for those who desire to enter the Direct Selling Profession and the children of direct sellers. The Foundation also provides education about the Direct Selling Profession at high schools, colleges and employment services throughout North America.

If you've ever had a thought or have been inspired to create the life of your dreams, than we invite you to discover the Direct Selling Women's Alliance! [xlviii]

CODE OF ETHICS: To ensure that the Direct Selling Women's Alliance remains a safe and supportive place for all direct sellers, we strongly prohibit cross-recruiting.

All members will be asked to agree to the following:

- Never approach, solicit or invite another member or guest to consider or enroll with my direct selling company either at or following the event.

- To network in a spirit of mutual support and respect for each individual's choice.

- Conduct myself in a sincere and professional manner at all times.

Members or guests who violate this code will be asked to leave and barred from membership or participation in future DSWA events.

CHAPTER 16
WORLD FEDERATION OF DIRECT SELLING ASSOCIATIONS (WFDSA)

World Federation of

Direct Selling Associations

The WFDSA is a non-governmental, voluntary organization globally representing the direct selling industry as a federation of national Direct Selling Associations.

WFDSA History

Founded in 1978, the WFDSA is a non-governmental, voluntary organization globally representing the direct selling industry as a federation of national Direct Selling Associations.

Direct selling involves the marketing of products and services directly to consumers in a face-to-face manner, away from permanent retail locations.

Our membership consists of more than 60 national direct selling associations and one regional Federation, with one delegate from each association, as well as a number of regional and global officers, serving as the Board of Directors. [xlix]

Mission

The WFDSA mission is to build understanding and support for direct selling worldwide. The association supports direct selling companies and associations by:

Developing, maintaining and promoting the highest global standards for responsible and ethical conduct.

Advocating the industry's positions and interest with governments, media and key influencers.

Serving as a trusted global resource for information on direct selling.

Facilitating interaction among direct selling executives on issues of importance to the industry. [1]

OBJECTIVES

What They Do

The Federation pursues the highest level of ethical conduct in the global marketplace, fosters advocacy by partnering with government, consumer and academic leaders, and strengthens management of national and regional Direct Selling Associations. Programs and efforts include:

ADVOCACY

Public Relations

Federation develops strengthens and maintains relations with governments, consume leaders, academia media and other external groups around the world. It works with these groups to improve awareness and understanding of direct selling.

Research

WFDSA conducts third party research and collects data on the socio-economic impact of direct selling, public attitude and facilitates long-term industry reputation enhancement.

Industry Social Responsibility

WFDSA collects and proactively shares information on the industry's corporate social responsibility efforts, including community service, charitable contributions and cause-related marketing, to show case the positive impact that the industry has on the societies in which it operates.

APEC CEPI

The Asia Pacific Economic Cooperation (APEC) Consumer Education and Protection Initiative (CEPI) was launched in 1998 by the World Federation of Direct Selling Associations (WFDSA) and officially endorsed by APEC Small & Medium Enterprises (SME) Ministerial in Christchurch, New Zealand in April 1999. The goal of the CEPI is to promote consumer education and protection and responsible business practices among small and medium enterprises in APEC economies. It does this by providing technical assistance through planning meetings, seminars and hands-on training. The CEPI is a true public-private initiative that brings together consumer, government and business leaders to plan each CEPI program to the needs of the local market. Ultimately, the CEPI is a capacity building project that helps build consumer confidence and helps small businesses grow.

GWEE

The Asia Pacific Economic Cooperation (APEC) Global Women's Economic Empowerment Initiative (GWEE) was launched by WFDSA in 2011 and officially endorsed by APEC Small & Medium Enterprises (SME) Ministerial in Singapore in 2009[how could it be endorsed before it was launched?]. The program is implemented in partnership with Kelly School of Business Institute for International Business (IIB), Indiana University. The overall objective of GSWEE is to provide basic business skills training to women micro - entrepreneurs in the APEC region.

GSWEE capacity building efforts are in line with APEC SME Ministers cutting edge-edge priority that developing micro-enterprises and investing in women will help with the overall economic recovery and reduce poverty and inequalities in the APEC region. The GWEE is a true public-private initiative. Governments, women's organizations, academia and other stakeholders are working closely with WFDSA to implement the program in various countries.

Self-Regulation/Consumer Affairs/Academic Programs

The Federation conducts seminars on a national, regional and global level, bringing together public and private sector consumer protection leaders, government officials and academia to foster greater consumer education and protections efforts. WFDSA also subsidizes national DSAs in conducting similar activities.

ASSOCIATION SERVICES

Training

WFDSA provides instruction on efficient and proper management of a DSA and how associations may better serve their members through global, regional and national seminars and other educational offerings.

World Congress

The Federation hosts the World Congress of Direct Selling once every three years. World Congress provides a forum where direct selling executives from around the world can discuss issues of importance to the industry.

ETHICS

Codes

Federation administers, promotes and enforces the World Code of Conduct and implementing programs aimed at improving the self-regulatory activities of the Federation, local DSAs and SELDIA.

Global Regulatory Affairs

The Federation develops strengthens and maintains relationships with regulators in various markets and conducts government relations/regulatory programs on a national, regional and global level.

PUBLICATIONS

World Federation News

The Federation's quarterly newsletter contains articles on the international world of direct selling and updates on national activities from DSAs worldwide.

Legal Compendium

The WFDSA Legal Compendium represents summaries of laws and regulations governing the direct selling from over 40 countries.

CEO Council News

The chairman's periodic newsletter to CEOs on the state of the Federation and the direct selling industry.

Conference Reports

Summaries of discussions and findings of regional symposia sponsored by the Federation [li]

CODES OF ETHICS

Code of Ethics Toolkit

Introduction to the WFDSA Code of Ethics

WFDSA's Code of Ethics Toolkit – Follow the Code, Communicate the Code, Promote the Code was designed by the WFDSA Ethics Committee to educate various constituencies around the world about the best business practices and ethical standards of the direct selling industry.

This toolkit contains flexible tools for DSAs and their members to help them communicate and promote the Code to the widest audience possible. Whether you are a consumer, educator, public policy official, independent distributor or a direct selling company, we've got an exciting and instructive tool for you.

We realize that around the world, there are many outstanding examples of how the Code of Ethics is being effectively promoted to company employees, distributors, consumers and the general public. Many of those ideas could and should be incorporated into this toolkit. Therefore, we welcome additional ideas, thoughts and real life experiences that can help to enhance our toolkit!

Contributions:

WFDSA would like to extend special thanks to the following people who assisted in the completion of the toolkit: John Higson (Avon), WFDSA Ethics Committee Chair (2008-2011); Josephine Mills (Avon), WFDSA Assistant Treasurer (2003-2011); Tamuna Gabilaia, WFDSA Executive Director; Sandi Rowe (Avon) and Dominick Correale (Avon).

OVERVIEW OF THE WFDSA CODE OF ETHICS

The World Code of Ethics is a constantly evolving, enforceable standard of behavior. It is the cornerstone of the direct selling industry's commitment to ethical business practices and customer service. It is a mechanism that ensures independent salespeople and customers are treated fairly and respectfully. The World Code has global applicability as it applies in countries where DSAs currently do not exist.

In order for a DSA to become a member of WFDSA, it must adopt the minimum standards set forth by the Code of Ethics to the extent the requirements are consistent with the law in each particular country. Every DSA member company pledges to abide by the Code's standards and procedures as a condition of admission and continued membership in a DSA.

The national DSA's Code of Ethics is enforced by an independent code administrator who is not connected with any member company. The code administrator will do everything possible to ensure Code compliance and where complaints exist, has the power to decide on remedies. All member companies agree to honor the administrator's decisions. [lii]

Resources for DSAs and Member Companies

Get the most out of WFDSA's ethics toolkit by taking full advantage of the resources available to you. The resources provided below will help you in your efforts to follow, promote and communicate the Code to your member companies, to independent sales force, to consumers and other constituencies.

The Code of Ethics PowerPoint Presentation (PowerPoint file)

Code at a Glance Brochure

"Our Promise to Consumers" Handout

This handout shows what you should expect when purchasing from a direct selling company

"Our Promise to Direct Sellers" Handout

As an independent direct seller you should know your rights. Is your company treating you the way it should as required by the Code of Ethics? What can you expect from your company?

Wallet sized "What Direct Seller Needs to Know"

This wallet-sized brochure is designed to remind you of your responsibilities towards your customers. Customer satisfaction is a key to your business success.

Code of Ethics Q&A for Sales force

The following are Situations and Q&A based on the DSA Code of Ethics. They represent situations you may face while running your direct selling business. Respond to them based on how you would most likely react in each situation.

Procedure for Initiating Complaints

Code Administrator Directory [liii]

Information for Direct Sellers

The Code sets forth a number of provisions to protect the interests of those who choose to affiliate with a company as an independent salesperson. The information provided in this toolkit will help you understand your rights as a distributor of a company's products and/or services. It will also help you understand your responsibilities towards your customers.

Direct Selling Companies' Promise to Independent Sales force

As an independent direct seller you should know your rights. Is your company treating you the way it should as required by the Code of Ethics? What can you expect from your company?

What are your Responsibilities towards Your Customers?

This wallet-sized brochure is designed to remind you of your responsibilities towards your customers. Customer satisfaction is a key to your business success. (Wallet Sized "What Direct Seller Needs to Know")

Realistic Examples with Q&A

The following are Situations and Q&A based on the DSA Code of Ethics. They represent situations you may face while running your direct selling business. Respond to them based on how you would most likely react in each situation. (Q&Brochure)

- **Code of Ethics (entire text)** (PDF file)

- **Code At a Glance Brochure** (PDF file)

- **Code of Ethics Q&A**

- **Procedure for Initiating Complaints** [liv]

Information for Consumers

You can buy with confidence, when you purchase products from a direct selling company that is a member of your local DSA. Each DSA member company must adhere to a Code of Ethics, which protects you as a consumer. The information provided in this section will help you understand your rights as a consumer. It will also answer some general questions you may have about the direct selling industry. [lv]

Direct Selling Companies' Promise to Consumers

The information below shows what you should expect when purchasing from a direct selling company:

- "Our Promise to Consumer" Handout (PDF file)

- Code At a Glance Brochure

- Code of Ethics Q&A

- Procedure for Initiating Complaints

- Code Administrator Directory

CODE OF ETHICS RECOGNITION PROGRAM

Eligibility and Guidelines for DSA

To participate in the Global Code of Ethics Recognition program "*Follow the Code, Communicate the Code, Promote the Code*" a DSA must:

Implement minimum of five criteria from the three sections below but no less than one criteria from each section

Demonstrate that the criteria were implemented prior to the end of the calendar year

Commit to continue implementing the criteria through at least the next calendar year

Any DSA that complies with the minimum DSA criteria regarding the independent Code Administrator and the WFDSA compliant Code may participate in the program. To qualify as a "*participant*" DSAs should complete, on an annual basis, an application indicating that the requirements set forth for the initiative have been met. DSAs that do not comply with the minimum DSA criteria are temporarily ineligible to participate in the initiative. Each DSA's qualifications will be reviewed by WFDSA.

Participants for 2012 (for activities completed prior to January 1, 2013) will be recognized via various WFDSA media and events. DSAs may apply at any time but must submit the completed forms no later than January 31, 2013.

Recognition Criteria

To qualify for recognition under the Global Code of Ethics Recognition program, implement minimum of five criteria from the three sections below during 2012.

Section I–Communicate the Code

Publish the Code-at-a-Glance brochure (print, website, DSA newsletters, etc...)

Publish complaint handling procedure on the website

Publish contact information (email, phone, address) for the Independent Code Administrator on the website

Section II–Promote the Code to Member Companies

Require member companies to appoint a Code Responsibility Officer (CRO), who will serve as a liaison among member companies, DSA and the Independent Code Administrator and will be responsible for company's adherence to the Code

Conduct Code training for new / existing members

Require member companies to submit a plan, with their annual dues payment, of how they are promoting the Code

Section III–Promote the Code to External Constituencies

Distribute copies of the Code-at-a-Glance brochure (active link here) to government officials, consumer agencies, academia, media, etc...

Obtain a "seal of approval" by local government / consumer protection agencies that can be used on all DSA and member company materials along with the DSA logo

Include the Code-at-a-Glace brochure or reference to the Code (URL) on all DSA literature and newsletters and in all press materials / events

APPLY FOR RECOGNITION NOW!

Recognition Form for DSAs

Application for Recognition for DSAs under the Global Code of Ethics Recognition program *"Follow the Code, Communicate the Code, Promote the Code"*

The direct selling industry has been in the forefront of the world business community in exploring globalization of its business opportunities and in initiating a self-regulatory approach for supporting ethical business behavior through its Code of Ethics. But the existence of these Codes does not automatically guarantee results–Codes must be Followed, Communicated and Promoted. Hence, effective Code publicity and promotion by DSAs and their member companies are essential for the following reasons:

Increase awareness by the general public regarding the advantages of dealing with DSA members when buying products through the direct selling channel

Communicate the good practices of DSA members to the media and consumer organizations.

Distinguish DSA members from rogue traders and incentivize rogue traders to improve their practices thus improving the reputation of the direct selling industry

Give non-DSA members reason to join a national DSA and comply with its code

Improve the reputation of direct selling and the benefits of self-regulation in the eyes of governments and regulators

To encourage companies to not only promote the Code, but to go above and beyond its requirements, the WFDSA CEO Council approved this global initiative to recognize DSAs and their member companies who will implement the ways to promote the Code in a way that will increase public awareness of the Code and ultimately underscore the value of upholding each of the Code's provisions.

All companies whose DSA implemented the initiative are invited to participate in the recognition program and will gain recognition by completing at least five criteria outlined below. For those companies who are eligible for the recognition program, please ask your local DSA to send you the application form.

WFDSA Global Code of Ethics Toolkit and Recognition Program Participation Criteria for DSAs/Companies

Application Form for DSAs (Download in Word)

Application Form for Companies (Download in Word)

Applications Are Now Being Accepted for Activities Completed in 2012. [lvi]

WFDSA CODE OF ETHICS

As adopted by the WFDSA CEO Council on October 7, 2008

Preface

This Code contains guidance on the interaction between:

DSA member Companies and their existing and prospective sales representatives;

DSA member Companies and their sales representatives and Consumers of the Company's Products;

Member Companies as they compete in the marketplace; and

Individual Complainants, the DSA Code Administrator, and DSA member Companies.

1.   General

1.1   Scope

The Code contains sections entitled "Conduct for the Protection of Consumers," "Conduct Between Companies and MLM distributors," and "Conduct Between Companies." These three sections address the varying interactions across the spectrum of direct sales. The Code is designed to assist in the satisfaction and protection of Consumers, promote fair competition within the framework of free enterprise and enhance the public image of MLM/Network Marketing.

1.2   Glossary of Terms

For the purposes of the Code, capitalized terms have the following meaning:

Code Administrator: The independent person or body appointed by DSA to monitor a Company's compliance with the Code and to resolve complaints under the Code.

Company: A business entity that (i) utilizes a MLM/Network Marketing distribution system to market its Products, and (ii) is a member of DSA.

Consumer: Any person who purchases and consumes Products from a MLM distributor or a Company.

MLM distributor: A person or entity that is entitled to buy and/or sell the Products of a Company and that may be entitled to recruit other MLM distributors. MLM distributors generally market consumer products directly to Consumers away from a permanent, fixed retail location, usually through the explanation or demonstration of products and services. A MLM distributor may be an independent commercial agent, independent contractor, independent dealer or distributor, employed or self-employed representative, or any other similar sales representative of a Company.

Order Form: A printed or written document confirming details of a Consumer order and providing a sales receipt to the Consumer. In the case of Internet purchases, a form containing all terms of the offer and purchase provided in a printable or downloadable

146

format.

Product: Tangible and intangible consumer goods and services.

Recruiting: Any activity conducted for the purpose of assisting a person to become a MLM distributor.

1.3 Companies

Companies pledge to adopt and enforce a code of conduct that incorporates the substance of the provisions of this Code as a condition of admission and continuing membership in the DSA. Companies also pledge to publicize this Code, its general terms as they apply to Consumers and MLM distributors, and information about where Consumers and MLM distributors may obtain a copy of this Code.

1.4 MLM distributors

MLM distributors are not bound directly by this Code, but, as a condition of membership in the Company's distribution system, shall be required by the Company with whom they are affiliated to adhere to rules of conduct meeting the standards of this Code.

1.5 Self-Regulation

This Code is not law, but its obligations require a level of ethical behavior from Companies and MLM distributors, which conforms with or exceeds applicable legal requirements. Non-observance of this Code does not create any civil law responsibility or liability. With termination of its membership in DSA, a Company is no longer bound by this Code. However, the provisions of this Code remain applicable to events or transactions that occurred during the time a Company was a member of DSA.

1.6 Local Regulations

Companies and MLM distributors must comply with all requirements of law in any country in which they do business. Therefore, this Code does not restate all legal obligations; compliance by Companies and MLM distributors with laws that pertain to MLM/Network Marketing is a condition of acceptance by or continuing membership in DSA.

1.7 Extraterritorial Effect

Every national DSA pledges that it will require each member as a condition to admission and continuing membership in the DSA to comply with the WFDSA World Codes of Conduct for MLM/Network Marketing with regard to MLM/Network Marketing activities outside of its home country, unless those activities are under the jurisdiction of Codes of Conduct of another country's DSA to which the member also belongs.

2. Conduct for the Protection of Consumers

2.1 Prohibited Practices

MLM distributors shall not use misleading, deceptive or unfair sales practices.

2.2 Identification

At the initiation of a sales presentation, MLM distributors shall, without request, truthfully and clearly identify themselves; the identity of their Company; the nature of their Products; and the purpose of their solicitation to the prospective Consumer.

2.3 Explanation and Demonstration

MLM distributors shall offer Consumers accurate and complete Product explanations and demonstrations regarding price and, if applicable, credit terms; terms of payment; a cooling-off period, including return policies; terms of guarantee; after-sales service; and delivery dates. MLM distributors shall give accurate and understandable answers to all questions from Consumers. To the extent claims are made with respect to product efficacy, MLM distributors shall make only those verbal or written product claims that are authorized by the Company.

2.4 Order Form

A written Order Form shall be delivered or made available to the Consumer at or prior to the time of the initial sale. In the case of a sale made via mail, telephone, the Internet, or similar non face-to-face means, a copy of the Order Form shall have been previously provided, or shall be included in the initial order, or shall be provided in printable or downloadable form via the Internet. The Order Form shall identify the Company and the MLM distributor and contain the full name, permanent address and telephone number of the Company or the MLM distributor, and all material terms of the sale. Terms of a guarantee or a warranty; details and limitation of after-sales service; the name and address of the guarantor; the duration of the guarantee; and the remedial action available to the Consumer shall be set out clearly in the Order Form or other accompanying literature provided with the Product. All terms shall be clear and legible.

2.5 Literature

Promotional literature, advertisements and mailings shall not contain Product descriptions, claims, photos or illustrations that are deceptive or misleading. Promotional literature shall contain the name and address or telephone number of the Company and may include the telephone number of the MLM distributor.

2.6 Testimonials

Companies and MLM distributors shall not use any testimonial or endorsement that is unauthorized untrue, obsolete or otherwise inapplicable, unrelated to the offer or used in any way likely to mislead the Consumer.

2.7 Comparison and Denigration

Companies and MLM distributors shall not use comparisons which are misleading. Points of comparison shall be based on facts which can be substantiated. Companies and MLM distributors shall not unfairly denigrate any Company, business or Product, directly or by implication. Companies and MLM distributors shall not take unfair advantage of the goodwill attached to the trade name and symbol of another Company, business or Product.

2.8 Cooling-off and Return of Goods

Whether or not it is a legal requirement, Companies and MLM distributors shall offer a cooling-off period permitting the customer to withdraw from the order within a specified, reasonable period of time. The cooling-off period shall be clearly stated. Companies and MLM distributors offering a right of return, whether conditioned upon certain events or whether unconditioned, shall provide it in writing.

2.9 Respect of Privacy

MLM distributors shall make personal or telephone contact with Consumers only in a reasonable manner and during reasonable hours to avoid intrusiveness. A MLM distributor shall discontinue a demonstration or sales presentation immediately upon the request of the Consumer. MLM distributors and Companies shall take appropriate steps to ensure the protection of all private information provided by a Consumer, a potential Consumer, or a MLM distributor.

2.10 Fairness

MLM distributors shall respect the lack of commercial experience of Consumers. MLM distributors shall not abuse the trust of individual consumers, or exploit a Consumer's age, illness, lack of understanding or unfamiliarity with a language.

2.11 Referral Selling

Companies and MLM distributors shall not induce a person to purchase goods or services based upon the representation that a Consumer can reduce or recover the purchase price by referring prospective customers to the MLM distributors for similar purchases, if such reductions or recovery are contingent upon some uncertain, future event.

2.12 Delivery

Companies and MLM distributors shall fulfill Consumer orders in a timely manner.

3. Conduct Toward MLM distributors

3.1 MLM distributors' Compliance

Companies shall require their MLM distributors, as a condition of membership in the Company's distribution system, to comply with the standards of this Code.

3.2 Recruiting

Companies shall not use misleading, deceptive or unfair recruiting practices in their interaction with prospective or existing MLM distributors.

3.3 Business Information

Information provided by Companies to prospective or existing MLM distributors concerning the opportunity and related rights and obligations shall be accurate and complete. Companies shall not make any factual representation to a prospective MLM distributor that cannot be verified or make any promise that cannot be fulfilled. Companies shall not present the advantages of the selling opportunity to any prospective recruit in a false or deceptive manner.

3.4 Remuneration and Accounts

Companies shall provide MLM distributors with periodic accounts concerning, as applicable, sales, purchases, details of earnings, commissions, bonuses, discounts, deliveries, cancellations and other relevant data, in accordance with the company's arrangement with the MLM distributors. All monies due shall be paid and any withholdings made in a commercially reasonable manner.

3.5 Earnings Claims

Companies and MLM distributors shall not misrepresent the actual or potential sales or earnings of their MLM distributors. Any earnings or sales representations made shall be based upon documented facts.

3.6 Relationship

Companies shall provide to their MLM distributors either a written agreement to be signed by both the Company and the MLM distributor or a written statement, containing all essential details of the relationship between the MLM distributor and the Company. Companies shall inform their MLM distributors of their legal obligations, including any applicable licenses, registrations and taxes.

3.7 Fees

Companies and MLM distributors shall not require MLM distributors or prospective MLM distributors to assume unreasonably high entrance fees, training fees, franchise fees, fees for promotional materials or other fees related solely to the right to participate in the company's distribution system. Any fees charged to become a MLM distributor shall relate directly to the value of materials, products or services provided in return.

3.8 Termination

If requested upon termination of a MLM distributor's relationship with a Company, Companies shall buy back any unsold, re-saleable Product inventory, promotional material, sales aids and kits, purchased within the previous twelve months and refund the MLM distributor's original cost, less a handling charge to the MLM distributor of up to 10% of the net purchase price. The Company may also deduct the cost of any benefit received by the MLM distributor based on the original purchase of the returned goods.

3.9 Inventory

Companies shall not require or encourage MLM distributors to purchase Product inventory in unreasonably large amounts. Companies shall take reasonable steps to ensure that MLM distributors who are receiving compensation for down-line sales volume are either consuming or reselling the Products they purchase in order to qualify to receive compensation.

3.10 Other Materials

Companies shall prohibit MLM distributors from marketing or requiring the purchase by others of any materials that are inconsistent with Company policies and procedures.

Direct Sellers who sell company approved promotional or training literature, whether in hard copy or electronic form, shall (i) utilize only materials that comply with the same standards to which the Company adheres, (ii) refrain from making the purchase of such sales aids a requirement of down line Direct Sellers, (iii) provide sales aids at a reasonable and fair price, equivalent to similar material available generally in the marketplace, and (iv) offer a written return policy that is the same as the return policy of the Company the Direct Seller represents. Companies shall take diligent, reasonable steps to ensure that sales aids produced by Direct Sellers comply with the provisions of this Code and are not misleading or deceptive.

3.11 MLM distributor Training

Companies shall provide adequate training to enable MLM distributors to operate ethically.

4. Conduct Between Companies

4.1 Interaction

Member Companies of DSA shall conduct their activities in the spirit of fair competition towards other members.

4.2 Enticement

Companies and MLM distributors shall not systematically entice or solicit MLM distributors of another Company.

4.3 Denigration

Companies shall not unfairly denigrate nor allow their MLM distributors to unfairly denigrate another Company's Products, its sales and marketing plan or any other feature of another Company.

5. Code Enforcement

5.1 Companies' Responsibilities

The primary responsibility for compliance of the Company and its MLM distributors with the Code shall rest with each Company. In case of any breach of this Code, Companies shall make every reasonable effort to satisfy the complainant.

5.2 Code Administrator

DSA shall appoint an independent person or body as Code Administrator. The Code Administrator shall monitor Companies' observance of this Code by appropriate actions and shall be responsible for complaint handling and a set of rules outlining the process of complaint resolution. The Code Administrator shall settle any unresolved complaints of Consumers based on breaches of this Code.

5.3 Remedies

The Code Administrator may require the cancellation of orders, return of Products purchased, refund of payments or other appropriate actions, including warnings to MLM distributors or Companies, cancellation or termination of MLM distributors' contracts or other relationships with the Company, and warnings to Companies.

5.4 Complaint Handling

DSA and the Code Administrator shall establish, publicize and implement complaint handling procedures to ensure prompt resolution of all complaints. Companies shall also establish, publicize and implement complaint handling procedures under their individual complaint handling processes to ensure prompt resolution of all complaints.

5.5 Publication

All Companies are required to publicize DSA's Code of Ethics to their MLM distributors and consumers.

   * File a code complaint

   * Code administrators

   * Code administrators list serve

Explanatory Provisions

1.4 Direct Sellers

While "distance communications" (e.g. internet sales) are generally not considered "direct selling," subsequent or repetitive transactions engaged in by a direct seller are meant to be covered by the Code, regardless of whether they are distance selling.

1.7 Extraterritorial Effect

This provision is intended to promote uniformity of ethical business practices, standards and behavior on a global basis. Should a Company choose not to be a member of another country's DSA, membership in this DSA will guarantee that some standard will apply in the other jurisdiction.

When engaging in Direct Selling activities outside of this country, each Company agrees to comply with the provisions of the Code of the other country's DSA (if a member).

It is envisioned that if a Company is not a member of the other Country's DSA, the Company agrees to comply with the provisions of the DSA Code in which the Company is headquartered (if a member of that country DSA).

If the Company is not a member of the DSA in which it is headquartered, the Company agrees to comply with the provisions of this Code or any DSA country Code to which it belongs.

2.8 Cooling-off and Return of Goods

The DSA Code Administrator has the authority to make a determination of what is a deceptive, unlawful or unethical consumer or recruiting practice under the Code using prevailing legal standards as a guide.

Compliance with any particular law, regulation or DSA Code of Ethics provision is not a defense to such a determination by the DSA Code Administrator that a practice is deceptive, unlawful or unethical. For example, in a sale to a consumer, compliance with the law does not bar the DSA Code Administrator from making a determination that a particular sales practice is deceptive, unlawful or unethical and that a refund or compensation is required.

3.6 Relationship

The term "written agreement" includes documents provided electronically, so long as those documents are printable or in downloadable form via the Internet.

3.9 Inventory

This section is not meant to create additional administrative burden on those Companies that do not require and do not encourage inventory purchase in any amount, but have a business model where the Direct Sellers purchase Products only after they have received Consumer orders for Products.

The following should be taken into account when determining the appropriate amount of Product inventory: the relationship of inventory to realistic sales possibilities, the nature of competitiveness of the Products and the market environment, and the Company's Product return and refund policies.

3.11 Direct Seller Training

Ethics training may be accomplished through in-person training sessions, online training sessions, written manuals or guides, or audio-visual materials.

It is anticipated that Companies shall endeavor to provide ethics training at no or little cost. In any case, Companies should not use ethics training programs as profit centers. It is recognized that ethics training may be provided as part of a broader training regimen, which may have some cost.

Code of Conduct Complaint Handling Procedure

HOW TO FILE A CODE COMPLAINT

If you have a complaint against a Direct Selling Association (DSA) member company (or an individual direct seller representing a direct selling company) that is a member of a DSA, you can file a complaint. The complaint can be in response to any business practice you believe is a possible violation of the DSA Code of Conduct [http://wfdsa.org/world_codes/].

Here are the steps you should follow:

First, try to resolve the matter directly with the individual(s) or the company involved. Your complaint should be in writing, and should include the following information:

The date and details of the incident

The parties involved

The section of the Code of Ethics that you believe has been violated

A description of the efforts you have made to resolve the matter

The cost of the product involved, if relevant, including invoices or other supporting documents

A description of the actions the other parties have made to resolve the matter

The current status of the complaint

The remedy you believe should be applied Please provide sufficient time for the company or individual(s) to respond to your written complaint. Usually, 30 days is suggested.

If, after completing step 1 (above) the situation is not satisfactorily resolved, contact the DSA Code Administrator in the country where the alleged violation occurred. You should provide the DSA Code Administrator with the same information identified in step 1 (above). Every DSA has a Code Administrator that administers its Code of Conduct [http://wfdsa.org/world_codes/]

If your complaint is not resolved to your satisfaction after completing step 1 and 2 (above), you should send the complete history of your complaint, including responses from both the company and the local DSA to WFDSA at: info@wfdsa.org. WFDSA will contact the local DSA Code Administrator and the local DSA to gain an understanding of why the complaint has not been resolved.

The WFDSA Code provides extra-territorial effect. This means that you can still be protected, and file a complaint even thought there may not be a DSA in your country or the company in question is not a member of your country's DSA but belongs to the DSA of its headquarters.

Here are the steps you should follow:

Find out where the company is headquartered

Find out if the company is the member of the DSA where it is headquartered [http://wfdsa.org/membership_directory/]

Send the complete history of your complaint to that DSA Code Administrator as outlined in step 1 (above) [http://wfdsa.org/world_codes/].

If the company is not a member of the country's DSA where the violation occurred and is not a member of the DSA where it is headquartered, you should lodge a complaint with the government or consumer agency. [lvii]

CHAPTER 17
DIRECT SELLING ASSOCIATION (DSA)
UNITED STATES

DIRECT SELLING ASSOCIATION

The Direct Selling Association (DSA) is the national trade association of the leading firms that manufacture and distribute goods and services sold directly to consumers. Approximately 200 companies are members of the association, including many well-known brand names.

The Association's mission is *"To protect, serve and promote the effectiveness of member companies and the independent business people they represent. To ensure that the marketing by member companies of products and/or the direct sales opportunity is conducted with the highest level of business ethics and service to consumers."*

The cornerstone of the Association's commitment to ethical business practices and consumer service is its Code of Ethics. Every member company pledges to abide by the Code's standards and procedures as a condition of admission and continuing membership in the Association. lviii

DirectSelling411.com

This is an interactive website set up by the Direct Selling Association for the sole purpose of providing people with the correct facts about the Direct Selling Profession. lix

CODE OF ETHICS

Understanding the DSA Code of Ethics

The DSA Code of Ethics is the cornerstone of DSA's commitment to ethical business practices and consumer service. Every member company and pending member company pledges to abide by the Code's standards and procedures as a condition of admission and continuing membership in DSA.

The DSA Code of Ethics speaks to both the consumer and the seller. It provides that member companies may make no statements or promises that might mislead either consumers or prospective sales people. Pyramid schemes are illegal and companies operating pyramids are not permitted to be members of the DSA.

The DSA Code of Ethics is enforced by an independent code administrator who is not connected with any member company. The code administrator will do everything possible to resolve any complaints to the satisfaction of everyone involved, and has the power to decide on remedies. All member companies have agreed to honor the Code administrator's decisions.

The Code is a constantly evolving, enforceable standard of behavior for DSA members and a mechanism that does aid salespeople and customers alike in getting answers to many of their complaints. Thankfully, despite millions of consumer transactions each year, DSA receives relatively few complaints. That's a testament to the standards themselves and the pledge that DSA member companies make to abide by them.

Following are some commonly asked questions regarding the Code and its function:

How was the DSA Code of Ethics developed?

The Code of Ethics has been developed over many years to protect distributors and consumers from unfair and deceptive business practices. It addresses issues that have been identified over the years as areas for potential abuse by companies or distributors. The US Code of Ethics is in conformance with the World Codes promulgated by the World Federation of Direct Selling Associations (WFDSA).

What does the Code of Ethics mean for me if I'm a distributor for a DSA member company?

The Code sets forth a number of provisions to protect the interests of those who choose to affiliate with a company as an independent salesperson. There is an important and mutually beneficial relationship that exists between a company and its sellers. Direct sellers are a "volunteer sales force" in that they set their own hours and work habits. At the same time, the company provides sellers with the opportunity to build their own business without the tremendous start up costs involved in a traditional business. Read more about what sellers should expect from a direct selling company.

What does the Code of Ethics mean for me if I'm a customer who has made a purchase from a DSA member company?

At its inception in 1970 the Code of Ethics was created as a consumer Code - specifically speaking to the interests of direct selling customers. The Code was expanded in 1978 to address the relationship between companies and their sellers, but the consumer protection aspect of this self-regulatory document remains a critical component. Find out more about what consumers should expect from direct selling companies and their sellers.

What does it mean if a company is a member of DSA?

DSA is a corporate membership organization. Direct selling companies are admitted to the association following a minimum one-year review period during which time the company's business plan is reviewed to verify compliance with all provisions of DSA's Code of Ethics. At present, only companies with direct selling operations in the U.S. are eligible for membership. Companies considering beginning direct sales or companies operating only in foreign countries may consider subscriber status with the association. After acceptance into the membership, companies are periodically reviewed to ensure continued compliance with all aspects of the Code of Ethics. Important among the requirements of the Code are pledges to: buyback inventory from departing distributors, not engaging in inventory loading, not requiring unreasonable upfront fees, not making misrepresentations about their products or opportunities, not operating as a pyramid scheme and hiding behind the independent contractor status of their salespeople to avoid application of the Code. And when a company doesn't abide by these standards, it will be subject to the judgment of an independent Code Administrator who makes determinations that are in the best interests of the consumer and the industry – not necessarily the company. Even the best of us make mistakes, and DSA's purpose is to minimize those mistakes by creating standards and providing a mechanism to address them when they happen.

What does it mean if a company is a pending member of DSA?

Pending member companies are undergoing the minimum one-year review process and must abide by the DSA Code of Ethics during this period. A list of pending member companies can be viewed on DSA's Web site.

What does the member review process entail?

DSA's process for reviewing companies prior to becoming association members is a rigorous one. It takes at least one year for applicants to become members. During that year, DSA looks at company marketing materials, contracts, manuals, video and other items to ensure compliance with the DSA Code. Law enforcement agencies and others are contacted to determine what kind of consumer complaints and legal and regulatory actions have been lodged that might raise questions about the applicant. Periodically Unannounced visits to company meetings are conducted to help ensure printed materials and real world practices of the applicants are consistent. If there are any questions about the company or its marketing plan, or any complaints of which DSA has been made aware, the company must explain them. If they can't explain, or won't, their application will be deferred it will be recommended to the DSA Board of Directors that the company not be admitted to membership.

What if I feel a DSA member company or representative/distributor has violated the Code of Ethics?

If at any time a DSA member company representative/distributor or customer feels one or more provisions of the Code has been violated, the incident should be reported to DSA's independent Code Administrator. The Code Administrator will review the incident in question and prescribe a remedy based on his findings. DSA member companies are required to abide by all rulings made by the Code Administrator to maintain membership in the association.

What is the role of the "Code Administrator?"

The Code Administrator is a person of recognized integrity, knowledgeable in the industry, and of a stature that will command respect by the industry and from the public. The Administrator establishes, publishes and implements transparent complaint handling procedures to ensure prompt resolution of all complaints.

I filed a complaint but did not receive a response from the company within 30 days. What do I do?

If you are concerned a complaint did not reach a company or that a complaint has not been addressed, you can contact the Code Administrator. The Code Administrator's toll-free phone number can be found in the letter you received regarding your complaint. If you cannot find the number, or have not heard back within a reasonable time frame, please contact DSA at 202-452-8866.

Can I file a complaint against a direct selling company that is not a member of DSA?

No. Unfortunately, DSA can only hold member companies accountable to the DSA Code of Ethics.

I have a complaint against a member company, but I'm not sure if it's a Code complaint. What should I do?

You may review the provisions of the Code of Ethics to make your own determination of whether a potential violation has taken place or you can simply file a complaint with the Code Administrator. The Code Administrator is the ultimate arbiter of whether a violation has occurred. lx

The Code and Member Companies

Compliance with the DSA Code of Ethics is a requirement for membership in the Direct Selling Association. All applicants for membership must complete a minimum one-year pending period during which time the company's business plan is reviewed to ensure compliance with all provisions of the Code. After becoming an active member of the association, companies are required to maintain compliance with the Code as a condition of continuing membership.

Company compliance with the Code of Ethics makes a bold statement about that company's commitment to practicing the highest ethics in business. By doing business with a DSA Member Company, the field sales force and the ultimate consumer can be sure they are dealing with a company serious about providing quality and service at the highest levels.

Each DSA member company appoints one member of its staff to serve as the Code Responsibility Officer (CRO). This individual is primarily responsible for communicating the tenets of the DSA Code of Ethics to the corporate employees and ensuring that the tenets of the DSA Code of Ethics are communicated to the company's sales force.

Displaying the DSA logo is a privilege given only to companies that have made the commitment to honor the Code of Ethics required for membership in the association. It should be regarded not only as a pledge to do right, but a promise to make a situation right in the event a problem does arise. [lxi]

The Code and Direct Sellers

As a salesperson, you should expect a DSA member company to:

Provide you with accurate information about the company's compensation plan, products, and sales methods.

Describe the relationship between you and the company in writing.

Be accurate in any comparisons about products, services or opportunities.

Refrain from any unlawful or unethical recruiting practice and exorbitant entrance or training fees.

Ensure that you are not just buying products solely to qualify for down line commissions.

Ensure that any materials marketed to you by others in the sales force are consistent with the company's policies, are reasonably priced and have the same return policy as the company's.

Require you to abide by the requirements of the Code of Ethics.

Safeguard your private information.

Provide adequate training to help you operate ethically.

Base all actual and potential sales and earnings claims on documented facts.

Encourage you to purchase only the inventory you can sell in a reasonable amount of time.

Repurchase marketable inventory and sales aids you have purchased within the past 12 months at 90 percent or more of your original cost if you decide to leave the business.

Explain the repurchase option in writing.

Have reasonable start-up fees and costs. [lxii]

The Code and Consumers

As a consumer you should expect salespeople to:

- Tell you who they are, why they're approaching you and what products they are selling.

- Promptly end a demonstration or presentation at your request.

- Provide a receipt with a clearly stated cooling off period permitting the consumer to withdraw from a purchase order within a minimum of three days from the date of the purchase transaction and receive a full refund of the purchase price.

- Explain how to return a product or cancel an order.

- Provide you with promotional materials that contain the address and telephone number of the direct selling company.

- Provide a written receipt that identifies the company and salesperson, including contact information for either.

- Respect your privacy by calling at a time that is convenient for you.

- Safeguard your private information.

- Provide accurate and truthful information regarding the price, quality, quantity, performance, and availability of their product or service.

- Offer a written receipt in language you can understand.

- Offer a complete description of any warranty or guarantee. [lxiii]

CODE RESPONSIBILITY OFFICERS

The DSA Code of Ethics mandates that all pending and active members of DSA designate Code Responsibility Officers (CRO).

DSA Code of Ethics, Section B, 3 - Code Responsibility Officer

Each member company and pending member company is required to designate a DSA Code Responsibility Officer. The Code Responsibility Officer is responsible for facilitating compliance with the Code by their company and responding to inquiries by the DSA Code Administrator. He or she will also serve as the primary contact at the company for communicating the principles of the DSA Code of Ethics to their independent salespeople, company employees, customers and the general public.

Every year at renewal, companies are asked to reaffirm that selection or designate another individual for that task. As indicated in the mandate in the Code, the CRO is the point person for the Code within that company. They are responsible for all aspects of facilitating compliance with the Code. They are responsible for responding to all inquiries from the DSA Code Administrator. The CRO is also responsible for communicating the principles of the Code to their independent salespeople, company employees, customers and the general public.

Some Key Points of Focus:

- The CRO should have a good understanding of what is required by the Code with regard to the company and the sales force.

- The CRO should ensure that the company has procedures in place that properly inform and educate their sales force about obligations under the Code.

- The CRO should ensure that their compensation plan remains focused on the sale of products to end users.

- The CRO should ensure the 90% buyback provisions are being communicated and enforced.

- The CRO should ensure that the company maintains a link on the company website to the DSA Code of Ethics.

- The CRO should ensure that the company's sales receipts are "Cooling-off" compliant.

- The CRO should ensure that any claims by the company or the sales force about the company or the company's products or services are accurate and not misleading. [lxiv]

Worldwide Obligations

The U.S. DSA is a member of the World Federation of Direct Selling Associations (WFDSA) and also serves as the secretariat for the organization which is a federation of all national DSAs around the world. The WFDSA promulgates a World Code by which all member DSAs must abide to the extent the requirements are consistent with the law in each particular country.

The World Codes were most recently updated in 2008, and the U.S. DSA Board of Directors approved a number of Code amendments in September 2009, bringing the U.S. DSA Code of Ethics into conformance. See the World Codes on the WFDSA Web site.

The U.S. DSA Code of Ethics includes an extraterritorial effect clause which requires U.S. DSA member companies operating in a country where they are not a member of the local DSA, or where a DSA does not exist, to comply with the World Code to the extent it is not inconsistent with U.S. law. [lxv]

Code of Ethics in Action

Communication Initiative Encourages Active Promotion of Code of Ethics by Member Companies

The following 45 DSA member companies were recognized during DSA's 2012 Annual Meeting for their participation in DSA's Code Communication Initiative. The recognition was based on activities completed by each company from March 2011 through March 2012:

- 4Life Research, LLC

- 5LINX Enterprises, Inc.

- ACN, Inc.

- AdvoCare International, LP

- All Dazzle

- Arbonne International, LLC

- Avon Products, Inc.

- Belcorp USA

- Celadon Road, Inc.

- CUTCO/Vector Marketing Corp.

- DeTech, Inc.

- Dove Chocolate Discoveries

- Enagic USA Inc.

- FreeLife International

- GeneWize Life Sciences, Inc.

- Gold Canyon

- Hy Cite Corp.

- Isagenix International

- JAFRA Cosmetics International, Inc.

- The Kirby Company

- lia sophia

- LifeVantage Corp.

- Mary Kay Inc.

- Morinda Bioactives

- Nu Skin Enterprises

- Oxyfresh.com/21Ten Inc.

- The Pampered Chef

- Paperly

- Regal Ware, Inc.

- Saladmaster, Inc. (A Division of Regal Ware, Inc.)

- SeneGence International

- Shaklee Corp.

- Silpada Designs

- SimpleXity Health

- Simply Said, LLC

- SimplyFun, LLC

- Southwestern Advantage

- Sozo Global, LLC

- Symmetry Corp.

- Tastefully Simple, Inc.

- Team National

- Univera

- USANA Health Sciences, Inc.

- Viridian Network, LLC

- YOR Health

What is the Code Communication Initiative?

The third-party credibility compliance with the DSA Code of Ethics affords your company is one of the most important benefits of DSA membership. But are you taking full advantage of this important symbol of commitment to consumer protection?

For each consumer, independent consultant, legislator or regulator who knows about and understands the importance of DSA's Code of Ethics your company benefits. Won't you join us in actively communicating with key audiences about the Code of Ethics?

Creating awareness about the Code among both employees and sales force members is already a required activity under the Code's provisions – but now your company can be recognized for your coordinated, purposeful efforts in this area when you are designated as a participant in DSA's Code of Ethics Communications Initiative.

During DSA's 2012 Annual Meeting 44 member companies (see list above) were recognized for going above and beyond in their efforts to promote awareness of the Code – your company should be among them next year.

Participating in the Code of Ethics Communication Initiative is easy, and some of the things you already do may help move you closer to qualifying for recognition in 2013. Here's how:

Take a look at the 14 activities listed below - they range from inviting a DSA staff member to address your national convention to posting a link on your Web site to www.directselling411.com, DSA's consumer Web site. Complete just five qualifying activities by March 2013, submit the participation form by the deadline and your company will be recognized at the 2013 Annual Meeting and be invited to display the DSA Code of Ethics Communication Initiative seal on your Web site, catalogs, or other promotional materials. You'll be viewed among your peers as a company that has gone above and beyond to promote the fact that you pledge to practice the highest standards in business ethics – it's a competitive edge you can't get anywhere else.

Recognition Criteria

To qualify for recognition under the Code of Ethics Communication initiatives complete just five of the following 14 activities between March 2012 and March 2013.

- Post a clear and conspicuous link to the DSA Code of Ethics (directed to either www.dsa.org or www.directselling411.com) on the home page of the company website.

- Inclusion of the complete DSA Code of Ethics on the company website.

- A link to DSA's consumer site: www.directselling411.com on the company website.

- Inclusion of the links to the DSEF produced DSA Code of Ethics Online vignettes on the company website.

- Engaging a member of the DSA staff to give an industry presentation to key company employees (senior management, Board of Directors or majority share holders).

- Engaging a member of the DSA staff to give an industry presentation to members of the field sales force at a company-sponsored event.

- Providing a training program (administered by company personnel) on the DSA Code of Ethics for members of the sales force.

- Distributing copies of the Code of Ethics to members of the sales force at a company event.

- Distributing copies of the Code of Ethics to members of the sales force in a stand-alone mailing.

- Inclusion of the complete DSA Code of Ethics in the company's policies and procedures manual.

- Inclusion of an article about the Code of Ethics in the company's print or electronic newsletter.

- Including a "Code of Ethics Quiz" on the company's website that encourages sales force members to learn about their rights and responsibilities under the Code.

- Begin including in the company's start-up kit a copy of the DSA produced one page synopsis of the DSA Code of Ethics.

- The company's Code Responsibility Officer participates in the annual CRO conference call.

The Fine Print

Any DSA direct selling member company may participate in the program and qualify as a "participant" by completing, on an annual basis, an application indicating that the requirements set forth for the initiative have been met. Each company's qualifications will be initially reviewed by the DSA staff and then be verified by the DSA Code Administrator.

Participants for 2013 (for activities completed prior to March 31, 2013) will be recognized at the 2013 DSA Annual Meeting in Phoenix. Companies may apply at any time between April 1, 2012, and March 31, 2013, but must submit the completed forms no later than March 31, 2013. [lxvi]

Filing a Code Complaint

 If you have a complaint against a direct selling company that is a member of the Direct Selling Association (DSA) for any business practice you believe is unethical or illegal and a possible violation of the DSA Code of Ethics, we recommend the following available options.

First, contact the salesperson immediately and explain your concerns.

Second, if the salesperson cannot or will not correct the problem to your satisfaction, call or write the company and explain the situation and outline the steps you would like to see taken.

If the company does not resolve your problem and it is a member of the Direct Selling Association, you may wish to file a complaint with the DSA Code Administrator.

To file your complaint online, please fill out the online Code of Ethics complaint form. Your information will be sent directly to the DSA Code Administrator who will investigate the situation and contact you directly. Click here to find out more about what to expect after filing a Code complaint.

If you'd like to submit your complaint in writing, you may mail or fax it to the address below. Your complaint should include the following basic information:

- The date and details of the incident

- The parties involved

- If possible, identify the Code violation you believe has occurred

- Efforts you have made to resolve the matter

- List the amount and cost of product, if relevant, include invoices or other supporting documents

- Any responses the other parties have made to resolve the matter

- The current status of the complaint

- How you would like to see the complaint resolved or remedied

Send your written complaint to:

Code Administrator

Direct Selling Association

1667 K Street, NW, Suite 1100

Washington, D.C. 20006

FAX (202) 452-9010

The Code Administrator is independent, not connected with any member company of the Direct Selling Association. The Administrator will do everything possible in accordance with the procedures of the Code of Ethics to resolve the problem to the satisfaction of all parties. A copy of the complete DSA Code of Ethics is available here or upon request to the Direct Selling Association. The Administrator is empowered to determine appropriate remedies and DSA member companies have agreed to be bound by the Administrator's decisions. [lxvii]

The Facts about Direct Selling That You Won't Hear From Short Sellers

As the association representing more than 200 leading firms that manufacture and distribute goods and services sold directly to consumers, the Direct Selling Association (DSA) would like to set the record straight in response to questions raised about the direct selling business.

Contact

Amy Robinson

202-452-8866

arobinson@dsa.org

STATEMENTS

Direct Selling Association Addresses Market Manipulation by Short Sellers

Millions of Americans will be harmed by unfounded and inaccurate statements about direct selling

Dec. 20, 2012 (Washington, D.C) - Today the well-being of millions of Americans who rely on direct selling as a source of supplemental income was put at risk when Bill Ackman of Pershing Square Capital presented a short thesis on Herbalife (HLF), making numerous statements and assertions critical of the company and the direct selling model that were misleading and unsupported by solid data. This follows his announcement on Wednesday that he holds a substantial short position on Herbalife stock.

"I think these short sellers are either disingenuous, misinformed or both," says Direct Selling Association (DSA) President Joseph Mariano. "Either way, it's unconscionable that they are putting at risk the legitimate sales and entrepreneurial activities for millions of people."

"Herbalife is a member in good standing of the Direct Selling Association. All DSA members abide by a strict Code of Ethics which specifically prohibits pyramid schemes. Clear legal standards and definitions have been developed over the past 30 years to rigorously enforce that prohibition. DSA and its members have worked for generations against the scourge of illegal pyramid schemes. To that end, DSA has supported strong anti-pyramid laws throughout the United States and worked to ensure consumers don't confuse legitimate direct selling companies with illegal frauds. Some short sellers have recklessly put at risk decades of public education and consumer protection in an apparent attempt to drive down stock prices of publicly traded companies so they can profit."

"The accusations made today by Mr. Ackman are made even more egregious by the distraction of his promise to donate the proceeds of his short position to his own company's foundation," Mr. Mariano added. "He is trying to masquerade as a consumer protection advocate when in fact he is not only taking money from other stockholders but harming millions of hard working Americans who are earning money through direct selling."

Direct selling is a time tested and legal method of product distribution that is attractive to many different types of individuals because of the flexibility it provides. Most direct sellers were customers of the product before they started selling the products. After becoming a direct seller they continue to use the products. In fact, some people join the company only to buy the products at a discount – they never intend to sell a single product or recruit a single individual. However, this fact is never mentioned by critics because it is not consistent with their rhetoric that falsely suggests everyone who becomes a direct seller having a high profit motive.

"Unfortunately, direct sellers have been unfairly targeted by short sellers who are cashing in on the market turmoil they cause," added Mr. Mariano. "If there is any group that should be investigated by the Federal Trade Commission or the Securities and Exchange Commission it is the short sellers themselves. There is no accountability for the accuracy of their statements and their profit has been made the moment the stock price falls. It's an unconscionable situation that literally takes money out of the pockets of working Americans."

Fact Sheets

- The Direct Selling Business Model is Thriving

- Legitimate Direct Selling Companies Offer Many Consumer Protections

- The Difference Between Legitimate Direct Selling Companies and Illegal Pyramid Schemes

- The Facts about Internal Consumption

- White Paper on Internal Consumption and Pyramid Schemes vs. Legitimate Direct Selling Companies

- The Direct Selling Association Responds to Questions about the Purchase of Products by Direct Salespeople

QUESTIONS AND ANSWERS

Q1: What's going on? Why has Herbalife been the subject of falling stock prices?

Recently, Bill Ackman, the founder of Pershing Square Capital Management and prominent hedge fund manager, announced that he's been shorting Herbalife for months and called the company a "pyramid scheme".

Unfortunately, even though direct selling industry has definitively demonstrated the propriety of its code of ethics to the regulatory community, Herbalife's stock price fell as a result. Markets often react to misinformation and uncertainty, which is what we believe, is happening in this case.

Q2: Did Ackman reveal a widespread problem among direct selling companies?

A2: The direct selling business model is solid and strong. After falling slightly in the wake of the Great Recession, total industry sales grew nearly one percent in 2010 and are expected to show even stronger gains when 2011 numbers are announced in early June. Most publicly traded companies reported strong earnings and income in 2011.

Q3: If this isn't an issue, why is DSA getting involved?

A3: DSA exists to protect and promote the direct selling industry by educating policymakers, the business community and the general public about the nature of the industry and how it works; as well as ensuring DSA member companies behave ethically in all aspects of their businesses through enforcement of the Code of Ethics. Part of our job is to correct misinformation.

Q4: What is the difference between a legitimate direct selling company and a pyramid scheme?

A4: Pyramid schemes are illegal. They prey on unsuspecting victims by masquerading as legitimate direct selling companies using a multilevel compensation plan. Conversely, legitimate direct selling companies contribute to a vibrant marketplace by selling competitive, high-quality products and services and providing a sustainable source of income for those who choose to sell those products.

Q5: What measures does DSA have in place to protect consumers against pyramid schemes?

A5: Pyramid schemes are illegal and companies operating pyramids are not permitted to be members of DSA.

Every member company pledges to abide by the DSA Code of Ethics as a condition of admission and continuing membership in the Association. The Code speaks to both the consumer and the seller. It ensures that member companies will make no statements or promises that might mislead either consumers or prospective sales people.

Q6: What is internal consumption?

A6: Internal consumption is a term used to describe the purchase of products or services by direct sellers. Nearly 16 million Americans engaged in direct selling in 2011, some as full-time entrepreneurs seeking to build a business and some as part-time representatives hoping to earn a little extra money. Others sign up as representatives simply to purchase products or services for their own use at a discount and never sell to anyone else. Regardless of their income expectations, almost all direct sellers use the products themselves.

Q7: Is internal consumption a legal business practice?

A7: Compensation received by salespeople for products they themselves buy and use, and those bought and used by other salespeople within their organization, is a legitimate, legal and ethical practice and not evidence of any impropriety.

Q8: If internal consumption is legal what, then, is the concern surrounding the issue?

A8: The Federal Trade Commission (FTC) and DSA Code of Ethics aim to protect consumers against compensation systems that are funded primarily or exclusively by payments made for the right to recruit other participants. Compensation must primarily be based on the sale of products and services to the ultimate consumer—whether or not that consumer is also a seller of the products. We believe the law, and resultant anti-pyramid enforcement, to be quite clear and settled on this issue. [lxviii]

The Facts about Internal Consumption

The direct selling industry has been in the news recently as a result of inquiries by a prominent hedge fund manager.

The inquiries arose from a question about "internal consumption"—the products and services purchased by direct sellers for their personal use. Internal consumption is often misunderstood and mischaracterized, when in fact it is a perfectly legitimate part of direct selling. As the association representing more than 200 leading firms that manufacture and distribute goods and services sold directly to consumers, we at the Direct Selling Association (DSA) would like to set the record straight.

Internal Consumption Is a Legitimate Business Practice Nearly 16 million Americans engaged in direct selling in 2011, some as full-time entrepreneurs seeking to build a business and some as part-time representatives hoping to earn a little extra money. Others sign up as representatives simply to purchase products or services for their own use at a discount and never sell to anyone else. Regardless of their income expectations, almost all direct sellers use the products themselves. This is what is known as internal consumption.

As the Federal Trade Commission (FTC) stated in a January 2004 Staff Advisory Opinion, internal consumption is not considered to indicate impropriety. Instead, "the critical question for the FTC is whether the revenues that primarily support the commissions paid to all participants are generated from purchases of goods and services that are not simply incidental to the purchase of the right to participate in a money-making venture."

In short, what the FTC watches for—and what the DSA Code of Ethics is designed to protect against—are compensation systems that are funded primarily or exclusively by payments made for the right to recruit other participants. Compensation must primarily be based on the sale of products and services to the ultimate consumer—whether or not that consumer is also a seller of the products. We believe the law, and resultant anti-pyramid enforcement, to be quite clear and settled on this issue compensation received by salespeople for products they themselves buy and use, and those bought and used by other salespeople within their organization, are a legitimate, legal and ethical practice and not evidence of any impropriety.

The Myth of the "70 Percent Rule"

We call the "70 Percent Rule" a myth because it isn't an actual rule. Instead, it represents an industry-adopted practice. The "rule" was first cited in 1979 when the FTC definitively determined that Amway was not a pyramid scheme. Among the evidence cited was the fact that company policy required 70 percent of inventory purchased during the past month to have been sold in order to qualify for compensation.

Illegal pyramid schemes often disguise themselves by encouraging "inventory loading" —convincing people to buy large amounts of inventory which they cannot easily sell to others and are not returnable. The FTC found Amway's "70 percent" requirement to be helpful in demonstrating that compensation was based on sales, not recruitment, and that no inventory loading was taking place.

Since that decision in 1979, many other companies have proactively adopted policies similar to the one Amway had in place. Additionally, there have been cases when law enforcement has taken action against an alleged pyramid scheme, ultimately requiring the company in question to adopt a version of this policy in order to continue to operate as legitimate, reformed operations.

The percentage of internal consumption varies by company, and regardless of the level it is not an indicator of a company's overall financial performance or health. The same is true of the "70 Percent Rule"—some companies adopt it, some don't. Importantly, DSA members also must abide by the Code of Ethics designed to protect both representatives and consumers.

Millions of Americans and people around the world benefit from the income they make through direct selling and enjoy the products they purchase. Direct sellers are the original word-of-mouth marketers—using personal recommendations to connect people and products. In a time when social media makes word-of-mouth a preferred method of gathering information and making purchasing decisions, direct selling couldn't be more relevant. [lxix]

DSA'S CODE OF ETHICS

Preamble

The Direct Selling Association, recognizing that companies engaged in direct selling assume certain responsibilities toward customers arising out of the personal-contact method of distribution of their products and services, hereby sets forth the basic fair and ethical principles and practices to which member companies of the association will continue to adhere in the conduct of their business.

Code of Conduct

1. Deceptive or Unlawful Consumer or Recruiting Practices

a. No member company of the Association or independent salesperson for a member company shall engage in any deceptive, false, unethical or unlawful consumer or recruiting practice. Member companies shall ensure that no statements, promises or testimonials are made that are likely to mislead consumers or prospective salespeople.

b. Member companies and their independent salespeople must comply with all requirements of law. While this Code does not restate all legal obligations, compliance with all pertinent laws by member companies and their independent salespeople is a condition of acceptance by and continuing membership in DSA.

c. Member companies shall conduct their activities toward other members in compliance with this Code and all pertinent laws.

d. Information provided by member companies and their independent salespeople to prospective or current independent salespeople concerning the opportunity and related rights and obligations shall be accurate and complete. Member companies and their independent salespeople shall not make any factual representation to prospective independent salespeople that cannot be verified or make any promise that cannot be fulfilled.

Member companies and their independent salespeople shall not present any selling opportunity to any prospective independent salesperson in a false, deceptive or misleading manner.

e. Member companies and their independent salespeople shall not induce a person to purchase products or services based upon the representation that a consumer can recover all or part of the purchase price by referring prospective consumers, if such reductions or recovery are violative of applicable referral sales laws.

f. Member companies shall provide to their independent salespeople either a written agreement to be signed by both the member company and the independent salesperson, or a written statement containing the essential details of the relationship between the independent salesperson and the member company. Member companies shall inform their independent salespeople of their legal obligations, including their responsibility to handle any applicable licenses, registrations and taxes.

g. Member companies shall provide their independent salespeople with periodic accounts including, as applicable, sales, purchases, details of earnings, commissions, bonuses, discounts, deliveries, cancellations and other relevant data, in accordance with the member company's arrangement with the independent salesperson. All monies due shall be paid and any withholdings made in a commercially reasonable manner.

h. Independent salespeople shall respect any lack of commercial experience of consumers. Independent salespeople shall not abuse the trust of individual consumers, or exploit a consumer's age, illness, handicap, lack of understanding or unfamiliarity with a language.

1a. This section does not bring "proselytizing" or "sales force raiding" disputes under the Code's jurisdiction, unless such disputes involve allegations of deceptive, unethical or unlawful recruiting practices or behaviors aimed at potential salespeople. In those cases, the section applies. As used in this section, "unethical" means violative of the U.S. DSA Code of Ethics.

The DSA Code Administrator has the authority to make a determination of what is a deceptive, unlawful or unethical consumer or recruiting practice under the Code using prevailing legal standards as a guide. Compliance with any particular law, regulation or DSA Code of Ethics provision is not a defense to such a determination by the DSA Code Administrator that a practice is deceptive, unlawful or unethical. For example, in a sale to a consumer, compliance with the Federal Trade Commission Cooling-Off Rule does not bar the DSA Code Administrator from making a determination that a particular sales practice is deceptive, unlawful or unethical and that a refund or compensation is required.

1. and 2. These sections cover communications about your own company or another company. For example, a distributor for company A makes misleading statements about company B and/or its products to consumers or prospective salespeople.

2. Products, Services and Promotional Materials

a. The offer of products or services for sale by member companies of the Association shall be accurate and truthful as to price, grade, quality, make, value, performance, quantity, currency of model and availability. A consumer's order for products and services shall be fulfilled in a timely manner.

b. Member companies shall not make misleading comparisons of another company's direct selling opportunity, products or services. Any comparison must be based on facts that can be objectively substantiated. Member companies shall not denigrate any other member company, business, product or service – directly or by implication – in a false or misleading manner and shall not take unfair advantage of the goodwill attached to the trade name and symbol of any company, business, product or service.

c. Promotional literature, advertisements and mailings shall not contain product descriptions, claims, photos or illustrations that are false, deceptive or misleading. (Promotional literature shall contain the name and address or telephone number of the member company and may include the telephone number of the individual independent salesperson).

d. Independent salespeople shall offer consumers accurate information regarding: price, credit terms; terms of payment; a cooling-off period, including return policies; terms of guarantee; after-sales service; and delivery dates. Independent salespeople shall give understandable and accurate answers to questions from consumers. To the extent claims are made with respect to products, independent salespeople shall make only those product claims authorized by the member company.

3. Terms of Sale

a. A written order or receipt shall be delivered to the customer at or prior to the time of the initial sale. In the case of a sale made through the mail, telephone, Internet, or other non face-to-face means, a copy of the order form shall have been previously provided, be included in the initial order, or be provided in printable or downloadable form through the Internet. The order form must set forth clearly, legibly and unambiguously:

Terms and conditions of sale, including the total amount the consumer will be required to pay, including all interest, service charges and fees, and other costs and expenses as required by federal and state law;

Identity of the member company and the independent salesperson, and contain the full name, permanent address and telephone number of the member company or the independent salesperson, and all material terms of the sale; and

Terms of a guarantee or a warranty, details and any limitations of after-sales service, the name and address of the guarantor, the length of the guarantee, and the remedial action available to the consumer. Alternatively, this information may be provided with other accompanying literature provided with the product or service.

b. Member companies and their salespeople shall offer a written, clearly stated cooling off period permitting the consumer to withdraw from a purchase order within a minimum of three days from the date of the purchase transaction and receive a full refund of the purchase price.

c. Member companies and their independent salespeople offering a right of return, whether or not conditioned upon certain events, shall provide it in writing.

4. Warranties and Guarantees

The terms of any warranty or guarantee offered by the seller in connection with the sale shall be furnished to the buyer in a manner that fully conforms to federal and state warranty and guarantee laws and regulations. The manufacturer, distributor and/or seller shall fully and promptly perform in accordance with the terms of all warranties and guarantees offered to consumers.

5. Identification and Privacy

a. At the beginning of sales presentations independent salespeople shall truthfully and clearly identify themselves, their company, the nature of their company's products or services, and the reason for the solicitation. Contact with the consumer shall be made in a polite manner and during reasonable hours. A demonstration or sales presentation shall stop upon the consumer's request.

b. Member companies and independent salespeople shall take appropriate steps to safeguard the protection of all private information provided by a consumer, a prospective consumer, or other independent salespeople.

6. Pyramid Schemes

For the purpose of this Code, pyramid or endless chain schemes shall be considered consumer transactions actionable under this Code. The Code Administrator shall determine whether such pyramid or endless chain schemes constitute a violation of this Code in accordance with applicable federal, state and/or local law or regulation.

6. The definition of an "illegal pyramid" is based upon existing standards of law as reflected in the matter of Amway, 93 FTC 618 (1979) and the anti-pyramid laws of Kentucky, Louisiana, Montana, Oklahoma, and Texas. In accordance with these laws, member companies shall remunerate direct sellers primarily on the basis of sales of products, including services, purchased by any person for actual use or consumption. Such remuneration may include compensation based on sales to individual direct sellers for their own actual use or consumption.

7. Inventory Purchases

a. Any member company with a marketing plan that involves selling products directly or indirectly to independent salespeople shall clearly state, in its recruiting literature, sales manual, or contract with the independent salespeople, that the company will repurchase on reasonable commercial terms currently marketable inventory, in the possession of that salesperson and purchased by that salesperson for resale prior to the date of termination of the salesperson's business relationship with the company or its independent salespeople. For purposes of this Code, "reasonable commercial terms" shall include the repurchase of marketable inventory within twelve (12) months from the salesperson's date of purchase at not less than 90 percent of the salesperson's original net cost less appropriate set offs and legal claims, if any. For purposes of this Code, products shall not be considered "currently marketable" if returned for repurchase after the products' commercially reasonable usable or shelf life period has passed; nor shall products be considered "currently marketable" if the company clearly discloses to salespeople prior to purchase that the products are seasonal, discontinued, or special promotion products and are not subject to the repurchase obligation.

7a. the purpose of the buyback is to eliminate the potential harm of "inventory loading;" i.e., the practice of loading up salespeople with inventory they are unable or unlikely to be able to sell or use within a reasonable time period. Inventory loading has historically been accomplished by giving sellers financial incentives for sales without regard to ultimate sales to or use by actual consumers. The repurchase provisions of the Code are meant to deter inventory loading and to protect distributors from financial harm which might result from inventory loading.

"Inventory" is considered to include both tangible and intangible product; i.e., both goods and services. "Current marketability" of inventory shall be determined on the basis of the specific condition of the product. Factors to be considered by the Code Administrator when determining "current marketability" are condition of the goods and whether or not the products have been used or opened.

Changes in marketplace demand, product formulation, or labeling are not sufficient grounds for a claim by the company that a product is no longer "marketable." Nor does the ingestible nature of certain products limit per se the current marketability of those products. Government regulation which may arguably restrict or limit the ultimate resalability of a product does not limit its "current marketability" for purposes of the Code.

State statutes mandate that certain buyback provisions required by law must be described in a direct seller's contract. While acknowledging that the contract is probably the most effective place for such information, the DSA Code allows for placement of the provision in either "recruiting literature or contract." The DSA Code is meant to emphasize that the disclosure must be in writing and be clearly stated. Wherever disclosed, the buyback requirement shall be construed as a contractual obligation of the company.

A company shall not place any unreasonable (e.g., procedural) impediments in the way of salespeople seeking to sell back products to the company.

The buyback process should be as efficient as possible and designed to facilitate buyback of products. The buyback provisions apply to all terminating distributors who otherwise qualify for such repurchase, including distributors who are not new to a particular company, or those who have left a company to sell for another company.

b. Any member company with a marketing plan which requires independent salespeople to purchase company-produced promotional materials, sales aids or kits shall clearly state, in its recruiting literature, sales manual or contract with the independent salespeople, that the company will repurchase these items on reasonable commercial terms.

Any member company with a marketing plan which provides its independent salespeople with any financial benefit related to the sales of company-produced promotional materials, sales aids or kits shall clearly state, in its recruiting literature, sales manual or contract with the independent salespeople, that the company will repurchase, on reasonable commercial terms, currently marketable company-produced promotional materials, sales aids or kits.

A member company shall clearly state in its recruiting literature, sales manual or contract with the independent salespeople if any items not otherwise covered by this Section are ineligible for repurchase by the company.

7b. 1998 amendments made it clear that sales aids, kits and promotional materials, while not inventory or necessarily intended for resale, are subject to the repurchase requirement if a company requires their purchase or if there is a financial incentive associated with their sale. It was recognized that "loading" of these items can cause the same harm to plan participants as loading of "inventory."

With respect to the final paragraph of Section 7b., disclosure of an item's eligibility or ineligibility for the buyback is key. Provided that repurchase is not required by this Code provision, for those items a company chooses not to repurchase, the company should clearly and conspicuously disclose to the buyer that the items are not subject to the repurchase requirement. Under such disclosure, a refusal to take an item back will not constitute a violation providing the member is acting in good faith and not attempting to evade the repurchase requirement.

8. Earnings Representations

No member company shall misrepresent the actual or potential sales or earnings of its independent salespeople. Any earnings or sales representations that are made by member companies shall be based on documented facts.

8. There is ample legal precedent in the form of FTC decisions to afford guidance on the subject of earnings representations. While not controlling, these precedents should be used by the Code Administrator in making determinations as to the substantiation of company earnings claims.

The Code's simple prohibition of misrepresentations was intended, in part, to avoid unduly encumbering start-up companies that have little or no actual earnings history with their compensation plan or established companies that are testing or launching new compensation plans. The prohibition approach is meant to require that companies in these circumstances need only ensure that their promotional literature and public statements clearly indicate that the compensation plan is new and that any charts, illustrations and stated examples of income under the plan are potential in nature and not based upon the actual performance of any individual(s).

9. Inventory Loading

A member company shall not require or encourage an independent salesperson to purchase inventory in an amount which unreasonably exceeds that which can be expected to be resold and/or consumed within a reasonable period of time. Member companies shall take reasonable steps to ensure that independent salespeople receiving compensation for down line sales volume are consuming, using or reselling the products and services they purchase in order to qualify to receive compensation.

9. See, Code Explanatory §7a. regarding inventory loading.

10. Payment of Fees

Neither member companies nor their independent salespeople shall ask individuals to assume unreasonably high entrance fees, training fees, franchise fees, fees for promotional materials or other fees related solely to the right to participate in the direct selling business. Any fees charged to become an independent salesperson shall relate directly to the value of materials, products or services provided in return.

10. High entrance fees can be an element of pyramid schemes, in which individuals are encouraged to expend large upfront costs, without receiving product of like value. These fees then become the mechanism driving the pyramid and placing participants at risk of

financial harm. Some state laws have requirements that fees be returned similar to the repurchase provisions delineated in Code §7a. The Code eliminates the harm of large fees by prohibiting unreasonably high fees. The Code Administrator is empowered to determine when a fee is "unreasonably high." For example, if a refund is offered for only a portion of an entrance fee, to cover what could be described as inventory, and there is nothing else given or received for the balance of the entrance fee, such as a training program, that portion of the entrance fee may be deemed to be unreasonably high by the Code Administrator. This Code section reinforces the provision in Code Part B. Responsibilities and Duties requiring companies to address the Code violations of their independent contractor sales force.

11. Training and Materials

a. Member companies shall provide adequate training to enable independent salespeople to operate ethically.

b. Member companies shall prohibit their independent salespeople from marketing or requiring the purchase by others of any materials that are inconsistent with the member company's policies and procedures.

c. Independent salespeople selling member company-approved promotional or training materials, whether in hard copy or electronic form, shall:

Use only materials that comply with the same standards used by the member company,

Not make the purchase of such materials a requirement of other independent salespeople,

Provide such materials at not more than the price at which similar material is available generally in the marketplace, and

Offer a written return policy that is the same as the return policy of the member company the independent salesperson represents.

d. Member companies shall take diligent, reasonable steps to ensure that promotional or training materials produced by their independent salespeople comply with the provisions of this Code and are not false, misleading or deceptive.

B. Responsibilities and Duties

1. Prompt Investigation and No Independent Contractor Defense

a. Member companies shall establish, publicize and implement complaint handling procedures to ensure prompt resolution of all complaints.

b. In the event any consumer shall complain that the salesperson or representative offering for sale the products or services of a member company has engaged in any improper course of conduct pertaining to the sales presentation of its goods or services, the member company shall promptly investigate the complaint and shall take such steps as it may find appropriate and necessary under the circumstances to cause the redress of any wrongs which its investigation discloses to have been committed.

c. Member companies will be considered responsible for Code violations by their solicitors and representatives where the Administrator finds, after considering all the facts that a violation of the Code has occurred. For the purposes of this Code, in the interest of fostering consumer protection, companies shall voluntarily not raise the independent contractor status of salespersons distributing their products or services under its trademark or trade name as a defense against Code violation allegations and such action shall not be construed to be a waiver of the companies' right to raise such defense under any other circumstance.

d. The members subscribing to this Code recognize that its success will require diligence in creating awareness among their employees and/or the independent wholesalers and retailers marketing the member's products or services of the member's obligations under the Code. No subscribing party shall in any way attempt to persuade, induce or coerce another party to breach this Code, and the subscribers hereto agree that the inducing of the breach of this Code is considered a violation of the Code.

e. Individual salespeople are not bound directly by this Code, but as a condition of participation in a member company's distribution system, shall be required by the member company with whom they are affiliated to adhere to rules of conduct meeting the standards of this Code.

f. This Code is not law but its obligations require a level of ethical behavior from member companies and independent salespeople that is consistent with applicable legal requirements. Failure to comply with this Code does not create any civil law responsibility or liability. When a company leaves the DSA membership, a company is no longer bound by this Code. However, the provisions of this Code remain applicable to events or transactions that occurred during the time a company was a member of DSA.

2. Required Code Communication

a. All member companies are required to publicize DSA's Code of Ethics to its sales people and consumers. At a minimum, member companies must have one of the following:

an inclusion on the company's web site of DSA's Code of Ethics with a step-by-step explanation as to how to file a complaint; or

a prominent link from the company's web site to DSA's Code of Ethics web page; or

an inclusion of the company's Code of Ethics, or its complainant process, in its web site, or with an explanation of how a complainant may appeal to the DSA Code Administrator in the event the complainant is not satisfied with the resolution under the company code, or the company's complaint process, with a reference to the web site of DSA's Code of Ethics.

a. The link should be clear and conspicuous. The location of the link on the company's website should be prominent so as to be accessible and visible to sales people and the consumer; companies should place the link on a web page which is commonly accessed by salespeople and consumers. Inclusion of a statement, such as, "We are proud members of the Direct Selling Association. To view the Code of Ethics by which we abide please click here," is also ideal. Companies should specifically link to either www.dsa.org/ethics/ or www.dsa.org/ethics/code/.

b. All members, after submission of their program, are required to state annually, along with paying their dues, that the program remains effective or indicate any change.

3. Code Responsibility Officer

Each member company and pending member company is required to designate a DSA Code Responsibility Officer. The Code Responsibility Officer is responsible for facilitating compliance with the Code by their company and responding to inquiries by the DSA Code Administrator. He or she will also serve as the primary contact at the company for communicating the principles of the DSA Code of Ethics to their independent salespeople, company employees, customers and the general public.

4. Extraterritorial Effect

Each member company shall comply with the World Federation of Direct Selling Associations' Code of Conduct with regard to direct selling activities outside of the United States to the extent that the WFDSA Code is not inconsistent with U.S. law, unless those activities fall under the jurisdiction of the code of conduct of another country's DSA to which the member company also belongs.

C. Administration

1. Interpretation and Execution

The Board of Directors of the Direct Selling Association shall appoint a Code Administrator to serve for a fixed term to be set by the Board prior to appointment. The Board shall have the authority to discharge the Administrator for cause only. The Board shall provide sufficient authority to enable the Administrator to properly discharge the responsibilities entrusted to the Administrator under this Code. The Administrator will be responsible directly and solely to the Board. The Board of Directors will establish all regulations necessary to administer the provisions of this Code.

2. Code Administrator

a. The Administrator shall be a person of recognized integrity, knowledgeable in the industry, and of a stature that will command respect by the industry and from the public. He shall appoint a staff adequate and competent to assist him in the discharge of his duties. During his term of office, neither the Administrator nor any member of his staff shall be an officer, director, employee, or substantial stockholder in any member or affiliate of the DSA. The Administrator shall disclose all holdings of stock in any member company prior to appointment and shall also disclose any subsequent purchases of such stock to the Board of Directors. The Administrator shall also have the same rights of indemnification as the Directors and Officers have under the bylaws of the Direct Selling Association.

b. The Administrator shall establish, publish and implement transparent complaint handling procedures to ensure prompt resolution of all complaints.

c. The Administrator, in accordance with the regulations established by the Board of Directors as provided herein, shall hear and determine all charges against members subscribing hereto, affording such members or persons an opportunity to be heard fully. The Administrator shall have the power to originate any proceedings, and shall at all times have the full cooperation of all members.

3. Procedure

a. The Administrator shall determine whether a violation of the Code has occurred in accordance with the regulations promulgated hereunder. The Administrator shall answer as promptly as possible all queries posed by members relating to the Code and its application, and, when appropriate, may suggest, for consideration by the Board of Directors, new regulations, definitions, or other implementations to make the Code more effective.

b. If, in the judgment of the Code Administrator, a complaint is beyond the Administrator's scope of expertise or resources, the Code Administrator may decline to exercise jurisdiction in the matter and may, in his or her discretion, recommend to the complainant another forum in which the complaint can be addressed.

c. The Administrator shall undertake through his office to maintain and improve all relations with better business bureaus and other organizations, both private and public, with a view toward improving the industry's relations with the public and receiving information from such organizations relating to the industry's sales activities.

D. Regulations for enforcement of DSA Code of Ethics

1. Receipt of Complaint

Upon receipt of a complaint from a bona fide consumer or where the Administrator has reason to believe that a member has violated the Code of Ethics, the Administrator shall forward a copy of the complaint, if any, to the accused member together with a letter notifying the member that a preliminary investigation of a specified possible violation pursuant to Section 3 is being conducted and requesting the member's cooperation in supplying necessary information, documentation and explanatory comment. If a written complaint is not the basis of the Administrator's investigation, then the Administrator shall provide written notice as to the basis of his reason to believe that a violation has occurred. Further, the Code Administrator shall honor any requests for confidential treatment of the identity of the complaining party made by that party.

2. Cooperation with the Code Administrator

In the event a member refuses to cooperate with the Administrator and refuses to supply necessary information, documentation and explanatory comment, the Administrator shall serve upon the member, by registered mail, a notice affording the member an opportunity to appear before the Appeals Review Panel on a certain date to show cause why its membership in the Direct Selling Association should not be terminated. In the event the member refuses to cooperate with the Administrator or to request a review by the Appeals Review Panel, the DSA Board of Directors, or a designated part thereof, may vote to terminate the membership of the member.

3. Informal Investigation and Disposition Procedure

a. The Administrator shall conduct a preliminary investigation, making such investigative contacts as are necessary to reach an informed decision as to the alleged Code violation. If the Administrator determines, after the informal investigation, that there is no need for further action or that the Code violation allegation lacks merit, further investigation and administrative action on the matter shall terminate and the complaining party shall be so notified.

b. The Administrator may, at his discretion, remedy an alleged Code violation through informal, oral and written communication with the accused member company.

c. If the Administrator determines that the allegation has sufficient merit, in that the apparent violations are of such a nature, scope or frequency so as to require remedial action pursuant to Part E and that the best interests of consumers, the association and the direct selling industry require remedial action, he shall notify the member of his decision, the reasoning and facts which produced it, and the nature of the remedy he believes should be effected. The Administrator's notice shall offer the member an opportunity to voluntarily consent to accept the suggested remedies without the necessity of a Section 4 hearing. If the member desires to dispose of the matter in this informal manner it will, within 20 days, advise the Administrator, in writing, of its willingness to consent. The letter to the Administrator may state that the member's willingness to consent does not constitute an admission or belief that the Code has been violated.

4. Appeals Review Panel

An Appeals Review Panel consisting of five representatives from active member companies shall be selected by the Executive Committee of DSA's Board of Directors. Each member shall serve for a term of three years. The five members shall be selected in a manner that represents a cross-section of the industry. When an appeal is made by a member company, the Chairman of the DSA Board of Directors shall select three of the five members of the Appeals Review Panel to constitute a three-person panel to review the appeal, and shall name one of them Chairman of that panel.

When possible, no company of the three shall sell a product that specifically competes with the Appellant, and every effort shall be made to avoid conflicts in selecting the panel. If for any reason, a member of the panel cannot fulfill his or her duties or fill out a term for any reason, the Chairman of the Board of DSA can replace that person with a new appointment for the remainder of the unfulfilled term with the concurrence of the Executive Committee.

5. Appeals Review Procedure

a. If a member company objects to the imposition of a remedial action by the Administrator, it shall have a right to request a review of the Administrator's decision by the Appeals Review Panel. A member company must make such a request in writing submitted to the Administrator within 14 days of being notified of the remedial action by the Administrator. Within 10 days of receiving such a request, the Administrator shall notify the Chairman of the Board of DSA who at that time shall select the three-person panel in accordance with Section 4 above. That selection shall take place within 30 days of the member's request for the review.

b. As soon as the panel has been selected, the Administrator shall inform the Appellant of the names of the panelists, including the name of the chairman of the panel. Within 14 days of that notification, the Administrator shall send a copy of the Complaint and all relevant documents, including an explanation of the basis of the decision to impose remedial action, to the panelists with copies to the Appellant. Upon receipt of such information, the Appellant shall have 14 days to file with the panel its reasons for arguing that remedial action should not be imposed along with any additional documents that are relevant. Copies of that information should also be sent to the Administrator.

c. Once the information has been received by the panelists from both the Administrator and the member company, the panel will complete its review within 30 days or as soon thereafter as practicable. The panel shall decide whether the Administrator's decision to impose remedial action was reasonable under all of the facts and circumstances involved and shall either confirm the Administrator's decision, overrule it, or impose a lesser sanction under Part E. The panel shall be free to contact the Administrator and the Appellant and any other persons who may be relevant witnesses to the Complaint, formally or informally as deemed appropriate. A decision by the panel shall be final and shall be promptly communicated both to the Administrator and the Appellant. The costs involved in the appeal such as costs of photocopying, telephone, fax, and mailing, shall be borne by the Appellant.

6. Codes of Ethics of Member Companies

a. Approval by Administrator

If a complaint is against a member company that has a code of ethics which has been registered with the DSA Code of Ethics Administrator, and the Administrator has issued an opinion that the company code is compatible with DSA's Code of Ethics, the Complainant must first exhaust all remedies under the company code of ethics before filing a complaint with DSA's Code Administrator. If the Complainant has exhausted those remedies and is of the opinion that the company's disposition of the Complaint was unsatisfactory, the Complainant can appeal the company's decision to the DSA Code Administrator. The Complainant must first notify the company of the intent to appeal to DSA. The Complainant must also forward all relevant documentation from the company code proceeding to DSA's Administrator.

After receiving such an appeal, the Administrator shall confer with the company to obtain any additional information concerning the matter as well as an explanation for the company's decision. The Administrator shall decide whether the company's resolution of the complaint was reasonable under all of the facts and circumstances involved. If the Administrator decides in the negative, the Administrator shall work with the company in an effort to resolve the matter satisfactorily to all parties. If the Administrator finds that the member company will not cooperate in that effort, the Administrator can impose remedial action in accordance with DSA's Code of Ethics. The Complainant shall bear all costs of an appeal from a decision under a company code, including such costs as photocopying, telephone, fax, and mailing charges.

b. Alternative Enforcement Process

In certain instances, a member company may provide a process whereby complaints can be addressed and which provide an equally acceptable vehicle for complaint resolution. In such instances – provided the process has been formally reviewed and approved by the DSA Code Administrator – the member company's process may be substituted for and the member company relieved of, adherence to the provision of Section D. Regulations for Enforcement of the DSA Code of Ethics.* In order for a member company's enforcement process to be approved as an alternative to Section D, the process must contain all the following elements:

The company has adopted an investigation and review process that substantially mirrors that presented in Section D and contains at more than one level the formal review of complaints regarding its salespersons or representatives;

The company has adopted an appeal process to the steps outlined in Paragraph 1 above that includes review by a neutral and competent third party, as approved by the DSA Code of Ethics Administrator;

The company offers a satisfaction guarantee or the equivalent on product sales to consumers who are not salespersons or representatives of the member company; and

The company advises its salespersons or representatives of the dispute resolution process in a sufficiently transparent manner including notices on its web site and in appropriate literature.

c. If a member company meets the above requirements of paragraph b., DSA will indicate on its web site that the member company's Code of Ethics is an approved Alternative taking precedence over the DSA's Code of Ethics Section D-Regulations for Enforcement of DSA Code of Ethics.

d. Those companies that are on the Company Code Alternative list will be exempt from the required publication provisions of Section B.2 of the Code and will not have to show on their web sites or in separate literature that complaints against the company should be filed with the DSA Code of Ethics Administrator. The DSA Code of Ethics web site will indicate, however, that all member companies are subject to all other provisions of the DSA Code of Ethics. Further, if the DSA Code of Ethics Administrator finds that any company on the Alternative list has failed to comply with the requirements for such a listing the Administrator may remove that company from the list.

E. Powers of the Administrator

1. Remedies

If, pursuant to the hearing provided for in Part D Section 3, the Administrator determines that the accused member has committed a Code of Ethics violation or violations, the Administrator is hereby empowered to impose the following remedies, either individually or concurrently, upon the accused member:

Require complete restitution to the complainant of monies paid for the accused member's products which were the subject of the Code complaint;

Require the replacement or repair of any accused member's product, the sale of which was the source of the Code complaint;

Require the payment of a voluntary contribution to a special assessment fund which shall be used for purposes of publicizing and disseminating the Code and related information. The contribution may range up to $1,000 per violation of the Code.

Require the accused member to submit to the Administrator a written commitment to abide by the DSA Code of Ethics in future transactions and to exercise due diligence to assure there will be no recurrence of the practice leading to the subject Code complaint.

Require the cancellation of orders, return of products purchased, cancellation or termination of the contractual relationship with the independent salesperson or other remedies.

2. Case Closed

If the Administrator determines that there has been compliance with all imposed remedies in a particular case, he shall close the matter.

3. Refusal to Comply

If a member refuses to voluntarily comply with any remedy imposed by the Administrator, and has not requested a review by the Appeals Review Panel, the DSA Board of Directors, or designated part thereof, may conclude that the member should be suspended or terminated from membership in the Association. In that event the Administrator shall notify the member of such a decision by registered mail and shall remind the member of its right to have the Administrator's original decision reviewed by the Appeals Review Panel in accordance with Part D Section 5 (Appeals Review Procedure) of this Code.

4. Appeal for Reinstatement after Suspension or Termination

If the suspension or termination is not appealed, or if it is confirmed by the Appeals Review Panel, a suspended member, after at least ninety days, and a terminated member, after at least one year, may request the opportunity to have its suspension or termination reviewed by the Appeals Review Panel which may in its discretion reinstate membership.

5. Referral to State or Federal Agency

In the event a member is suspended or terminated, and continues to refuse to comply with any remedy imposed by the Administrator within 30 days after suspension or termination, the Administrator may then consult with independent legal counsel to determine whether the facts that have been ascertained amount to a violation of state or federal law. If it is determined that such a violation may have occurred, the Administrator shall so notify the accused member by certified or registered mail, return receipt requested, and if appropriate action has not been taken by the accused member, and communicated to the Administrator after 15 days following such notice, the Administrator may submit the relevant data concerning the complaint to the appropriate federal or local agency.

F. Restrictions

1. Conferring with Others

At no time during an investigation or the hearing of charges against a member shall the Administrator or member of the Appeals Review Panel confer with anyone at any time concerning any alleged violation of the Code, except as provided herein and as may be necessary to conduct the investigation and hold a hearing. Any information ascertained during an investigation or hearing shall be treated as confidential, except in cases where the accused member has been determined to have violated federal, state or local statutes. At no time during the investigation or the hearing of charges shall the Administrator or a member of the Appeals Review Panel confer with a competitor of the member alleged to be in violation of the Code, except when it may be necessary to call a competitor concerning the facts, in which case the competitor shall be used only for the purpose of discussing the facts. At no time shall a competitor participate in the Administrator's or in the Appeals Review Panel's disposition of a complaint.

2. Documents

Upon request by the Administrator to any member, all documents directly relating to an alleged violation shall be delivered to the Administrator. Any such information obtained by the Administrator shall be held in confidence in accord with the terms of these regulations and the Code. Whenever the Administrator, either by his own determination or pursuant to a decision by the Appeals Review Panel, terminates an action which was begun under the Code, a record of the member accused shall be wiped clean and all documents, memoranda or other written material shall either be destroyed or returned, as may be deemed appropriate by the Administrator, except to the extent necessary for defending a legal challenge to the Administrator's or Appeals Review Panel's handling of a matter, or for submitting relevant data concerning a complaint to a local, state or federal agency. At no time during proceedings under this Code regulation or under the Code shall the Administrator or member of the Appeals Review Panel either unilaterally or through the DSA issue a press release concerning allegations or findings of a violation of the Code unless specifically authorized to do so by the Executive Committee of DSA's Board of Directors.

3. Pending Members of DSA

Nothing in Part F shall prevent the Administrator from notifying, at his discretion, DSA staff members of any alleged violations of the Code that have come to his attention and which may have a bearing on a DSA pending member's qualifications for active membership.

G. Resignation

Resignation from the Association by an accused company prior to completion of any proceedings constituted under this Code shall not be grounds for termination of said proceedings, and a determination as to the Code violation shall be rendered by the Administrator at his or her discretion, irrespective of the accused company's continued membership in the Association or participation in the complaint resolution proceedings.

H. Amendments

This Code may be amended by vote of two thirds of the Board of Directors.

As Adopted - June 15, 1970 - As Amended by Board of Directors through December 7, 2011[lxx]

CHAPTER 18
DIRECT SELLERS ASSOCIATION - CANADA

The Association

The DSA is devoted to preserving the integrity of the direct selling industry in Canada – whether working on behalf of member firms to address issues of importance, providing member companies and their ISCs with support through the DSA Rewards products, educating the public on the benefits of direct selling, or ensuring consumer protection by enforcing the high standards set out in the Codes.[lxxi]

Direct Sellers Association
Mark of Trust and Integrity

Consumer Protection

As a consumer in today's world, you like to be well-informed about purchases and suppliers. The Direct Sellers Association (DSA) embodies that same desire for healthy transactions, information transparency, and industry advocacy. So, to help ensure that you – the consumer – have the best possible purchase experience, we're pleased to share these resources in three (3) key knowledge areas:

- the DSA's own commitment and Code of Ethics

- earmarks for recognizing reputable firms; and

- how to get resolution, should you have a complaint. lxxii

CODE OF ETHICS

Because industry integrity is the cornerstone of the DSA, it upholds codes of ethics and business practices as pledges for companies and independents to follow in product sales, consumer care, and recruitment and sales force relations. Each member company must rededicate annually to these provisions, so rest assured, any salespeople of DSA member companies have committed to — among other assurances as are also outlined under Reputable Firms) tell you who they are and what they're selling; call at times that suit you, and respect your right to end a call; and

give truthful information on the price, quality, performance, quantity, and availability of their products or services.

There are 50 article codes in all, grouped to address target member sectors. Here, you'll see the Code of Ethics covers Articles 1-28, Business Practices cover Articles 1-17, and there's a Code Enforcement/Complaint Procedure section (A-E).

Code of Ethics

Articles 1-10 for DSA Member Responsibilities — Accuracy, Price/Credit Terms, Cooling Off, Guarantees, After Sales Service, Identity of the Seller, Clarity, Safety, Complaints

Articles 11-13 for DSA Member Company Independent Sales Contractors (ISCs) Responsibilities — Presentation of the Offer, Information

Articles 14-17 for Independent Sales Contractors (ISCs) Operations — Respect of Privacy, Honesty & Fairness, Veracity

Articles 18-28 for Active DSA Members and ISCs Joint Responsibilities — Testimonials & Endorsements, Comparisons & Fair Competition, Referral Selling, Delivery, Responsibility for Code Observance

Business Practices

Articles 1-8 for Independent Sales Contractors (ISCs). — General, Recruiting, Education, False or Misleading Statements, Disparaging Claims

Articles 9-17 for Active DSA Obligations to Members, Salespersons, Sales Policies, and Salesperson Relations — Active DSA Obligations, Recruiting, Education, Observance, General Responsibilities

Code Enforcement / Complaints Procedure

Interpretation & Execution; B) Code Administrator; C) Procedure; D) Extra-Territoriality; E) Amendments. [lxxiii]

DSA'S COMMITMENT

The DSA embodies all that is best in the direct sales field, and that is reflected in our commitment to enhanced professionalism and expertise in a competitive arena; clear, concise, ongoing communication; and member forums to discuss, develop, and implement programs to benefit the industry and individual business relationships. This climate helps to expand our presence as the principal voice of the direct selling industry, where we are proud to be perceived:

- by entrepreneurs as a viable career earning opportunity;

- by consumers as a reliable and credible supplier of quality products, services, and marketplace opportunities;

- by special interest groups as a positive, productive association that represents credible, reasonable views; and

- by Canadians as socially concerned, responsible, and involved with our Canadian society.

Each company must meet specific member criteria, ensuring their ability to live up to the high standards established by the DSA. A DSA Membership Application Review Committee conducts a routine investigation of the company's business reputation, including its marketing and distribution plan, to ensure compliance with federal and provincial laws. And finally, each member company must agree to abide by the DSA's Codes of Ethics and Business Practices, designed to protect customers and prospective entrepreneurs. [lxxiv]

RECOGNIZING REPUTABLE FIRMS

When it comes to direct sales, consumers are looking for a quality product or service, a fair price, and a guarantee they can trust.

So, how can you identify businesses that embrace these core principles? Look for the DSA logo on catalogues and sales materials. Like the Good Housekeeping seal of approval, the DSA logo serves as a clear identifier that the company you're dealing with is a member in good standing and has agreed to abide by the DSA's Codes of Ethics and Business Practices. You also want to find salespeople who will:

- say who they are, why they're approaching you, and what they're selling.

- clearly explain how to return or cancel an order

- honour your privacy by calling at times that best suit you, and

- respect your right to end a sales call.

- And, when you make a purchase, look for the assurances you can count on with DSA members:

- truthful information on the price, quality, performance, quantity, and availability of products or services

- a written receipt in clear language

- their own name and address, and that of the firm represented

- a full description of any warranty or guarantee, limited or full

- assurance that all testimonials and endorsements are truthful, current, and authorized by the person or organization quoted

- any product claims are based on substantiated facts.

- AVOID salespeople or companies who/that:

- disparage other products or suppliers

- confuse you, abuse your trust, or exploit your lack of experience or knowledge

- urge you to cancel a contract with another salesperson

- falsely claim you've just won a contest or that they're doing a survey.

- And certainly, avoid illegal pyramid schemes by reviewing our identifying red flags. Whether simple (similar to chain letters) or more cunningly disguised (like predatory wolves trying to fool investors and evade law enforcers), don't be their next victim. Be clear about what to look for in a legitimate, lucrative business opportunity. [lxxv]

COMPLAINT RESOLUTION

While it's rare that consumers find complaint with DSA members, we stand ready to assist you if the need arises. If ever you feel a DSA firm is engaging in a business practice you believe to be unethical, illegal, or violating our Code of Ethics (to which every DSA member must adhere), we recommend these steps:

- First, try to resolve the matter directly with the company. Your complaint should be in writing and include the following basic points:

- date and details of the incident

- parties involved

- if possible, identify the specific Code you feel was violated

- efforts you've made to resolve the matter

- cost and amount of product, if relevant, and include invoices or other supporting documents

- any responses the other parties made to resolve the matter

- current status of the complaint

- how you'd like to see the issue resolved or remedied.

If you still are not satisfied, contact the DSA's Code Administrator (C.A.), providing a written description of your complaint. The C.A. acts independently, and all member companies have agreed to honour his decisions. The C.A. is not connected with any member company nor Association staff, and you can correspond directly with the C.A. (marked "CONFIDENTIAL") via:

DSA Code Administrator,

c/o Direct Sellers Association of Canada,

180 Attwell Drive, Suite #250,

Toronto, Ontario M9W 6A9

Pyramid Schemes

NOTE: Pyramid schemes are ILLEGAL. Canadians lose millions of dollars every year to pyramid schemes, illegal scams in which huge numbers of people at the bottom of the pyramid pay money to a few people at the top. For this to work, for everyone to profit, there would have to be an unending source of new participants. But there isn't. In reality, supply is limited, so each new level of participants has less chance of recruiting others and a greater chance of actually losing money.

Some pyramids use a get-rich-quick sales pitch for investing, luring people and their money into illegal "investment clubs". Others are disguised as legitimate direct selling or multi-level systems, bilking victims who thought they were paying for help in starting their own small business. So, how can you tell the difference?

One big rip-off tip-off ... more focus on recruiting people than on selling products.

It's a red flag if anyone tries to entice you with unlimited wealth simply by recruiting more people into the scheme and/or payment of large, up-front "membership fees." Pyramid schemes will typically charge high "entrance fees," possibly buried in the cost of a starter kit, in startup inventory, or for training or other services. These proposals will concentrate on the importance of recruiting others to achieve high profits. Often, little or no focus is placed on the product or service they may claim to represent, or on the subsequent sale of these products and services to customers.

On the other hand, legitimate companies like those in the DSA concentrate on selling worthwhile products or services at competitive prices, often through home shows, providing a popular, low-cost way for you to start your own small business. So, before starting your own home-based venture in direct sales or multi-level marketing, ask three (3) critical questions:

What are the startup costs?

If they're substantial, be careful. Legitimate companies want to make it easy and inexpensive for you to start selling their products and services.

Will the company buy back inventory?

If not, you could be stuck with a roomful of unsold, unsaleable inventory. (DSA members adhere to strict codes requiring, among other things, that active members permit their salespeople to return products in saleable condition on reasonable commercial terms.)

Does the company have substantial sales to consumers?

If it's "NO", don't get involved! Multi-level marketing, like any other healthy business, is built on sales and service to consumers. Pyramid schemes concentrate on making most of their money from you and other new recruits.

Don't be rushed into a decision about starting your own business. And avoid any company refusing to answer questions about its products and services, startup costs, average earnings, etc. Remember ... pyramid schemes seek to make fast money from you. Legitimate firms want to make long term money for you and with you as you build your business by selling consumer products and services. That's the credo of the member companies of the DSA. [lxxvi]

GOVERNMENT RELATIONS

On behalf of its members, the DSA:

- stays abreast of legislative issues that affect direct selling,

- remains a constructive influence with policy makers by maintaining active relationships with key government portfolios;

- communicates to inform members of relevant issues through various channels and vehicles such as periodic action alerts, a legislative manual, and a municipal licensing registry;

- reviews member company marketing plans and documentation to ensure regulatory and government compliance;

  - helps to resolve industry concerns through lobbying.[lxxvii]

ISSUES ADVOCACY

As the voice for Canada's direct selling industry, the DSA positions many hot-button concerns on the radar of key levels of government through our Government Affairs Committee and its subcommittee for Taxation and for Health Canada.

Hot Topics

More recently, the DSA committees have been involved in issues that include:

- Bill C-51[lxxviii]

- the amendment to the Telecommunications Act reflecting the implementation of a national do-not-call list;

- the amendment to Cosmetic Regulations with the implementation of mandatory ingredient labeling;

- a proposal for a new Canada Health Protection Act that will replace the Food & Drugs Act, among others;

- tax requirements for independent sales consultants;

- and provincially, eco/environmental mandates on packaging, compensation for reclaiming residual materials, etc.

Meeting Summaries

DSA executives enjoyed positive, supportive meetings with the Prime Minister's Office and the Standing Committee on Health to unclog the backlog of registrations due to new, onerous mandates of the Natural Health Products Regulations.

Requesting a status update from the Therapeutic Products Directorate, the DSA learned there's no longer a prohibition on four (4) previously banned active ingredients in sun screens. We then advised members to review the revised monograph at Health Canada.

The DSA joined others in a coalition that met with a Federal Finance advisor to oppose a proposed net income test and the introduction of REOP.

The DSA, part of a government committee for Alberta / B.C., met to build a ground breaking internal trade agreement that also amalgamates legislation with the promise to include direct sellers.[lxxix]

ABOUT THE AUTHOR

Kevin McNabb is the Founder of Kevin McNabb International, Creator of The Responsible Direct Seller Series™, Creator of Adventures of Maya™ and Author of Ethics in Direct Sales.

Kevin began his Direct Selling (Network Marketing) journey in 1985 and has been blessed with the opportunity to help others around the world.

Kevin McNabb is one of the most in-demand speakers on ethics, peak performance, leadership, and responsible marketing in the North America.

Kevin has shared the stage with Kim & Robert Kiyosaki, John C. Maxwell, Robert Rohm, Lisa Nichols, Paul Zane Pilzer, Bruce Wilkerson, Chris Widener, Andy Stanley, Dexter & Birdie Yager, Rich & Doug Devos, Jay & Steve Van Andel, Burke Hedges, Ron Ball, Brad & Kim DeHaven, Scott & MJ Michael, Ron & Toby Hale, Joe & Marybeth Markiewicz, Bill & Janice Kerr, Lennon Ledbetter, Grace and Nicki Keohohou, , Frank & Joan Mazzeo, Mark Hughes, Randy & Valorie Haugen, Jim & Sherry Reed, Bill Childers, Tim Foley, George & Ruth Halsey, Jerry & Cherry Meadows, Ron & Georgia Lee Puryear, Jody & Kathy Victor, Rick & Sue Lynn Setzer and many more.

To learn more about Kevin McNabb, visit: www.KevinMcNabb.com

To learn more about The Responsible Direct Seller Series™, visit: www.TheResponsibleDirectSellerSeries.com

To learn more about Ethics in Direct Sales, visit: www.EthicsInDirectSales.com

COMING SOON

"Ethics in Direct Sales – The Rising of a Gold Standard 3.0 Life!"

Audio CD Program and DVD Program.

For more information, visit:

www.EthicsInDirectSales.com

END NOTES

i What is Direct Selling - http://www.directselling411.com/

ii World Federation of Direct Selling Associations, Global Statistics Report 2011, http://www.wfdsa.org/files/pdf/global-stats/Global_Statistical_Report_Final_6-20-2012.pdf

iii Federal Trade Commission, MLM – A Litany Of Misrepresentations, Page 1 http://ftc.gov/os/comments/bizoppstaffreport/00010-57283.pdf

iv Federal Trade Commission, MLM – A Litany Of Misrepresentations, Page 37 http://ftc.gov/os/comments/bizoppstaffreport/00010-57283.pdf

v Direct Selling Association, Code of Ethics, Proselyting, http://www.dsa.org/ethics/

vi Direct Selling Association, Code of Ethics, Proselyting, http://www.dsa.org/ethics/proselyting/

vii Direct Selling Association, Memo: Ethics and Self-Regulation Committee, http://www.dsa.org/ethics/proselyting/proselytingmemo.pdf

viii Federal Trade Commission, MLM – A Litany Of Misrepresentations, Page 4 to 10 http://ftc.gov/os/comments/bizoppstaffreport/00010-57283.pdf

ix A Project of ProEthics Ltd., Ethics Scoreboard, http://www.ethicsscoreboard.com/rb_definitions.html

x Executive Leadership Foundation, Inc., Absolute Ethics: A Proven System of True Profitability (Tucker, GA., 1987) 22-23

xi Epistle to the Son of the Wolf, 30, quoted at http://reference.bahai.org/en/t/b/ESW/esw-2.html , 11 May 2013

xii Udana-Varga, 5, 1, quoted at www.thegoldenrule.net, 11 May 2013

xiii Mathew 7:12, quoted at www.thegoldenrule.net, 11 May 2013

xiv Analects 15:23, quoted at www.thegoldenrule.net, 11 May 2013

xv A version of the golden rule put into modern, non-religious terms that some people live by, quoted at www.thegoldenrule.net, 11 May 2013

xvi Mahabharata 5, 1, quoted in ibid.

xvii The Traditions of Mohammed, quoted at www.thegoldenrule.net, 11 May 2013

xviii Sutrakritanga 1.11.33, quoted at www.thegoldenrule.net, 11 May 2013 xix Talmud, Shabbat 31a

xx quoted at www.thegoldenrule.net, 11 May 2013

xxi Shast-nashayast 13:29, quoted at www.thegoldenrule.net, 11 May 2013

xxii USAMutuals.com, quoted at http://www.usamutuals.com/vicefund/abt.aspx, 11 May 2013

xxiii Fortune Magazine, CNN Money, 100 Best Companies to Work For, quoted at http://money.cnn.com/magazines/fortune/best-companies/2013/snapshots/1.html?iid=bc_sp_list 11 May 2013

xxiv Google.com, quoted at https://www.google.ca/intl/en/about/, 11 May 2013

xxv United States Census Bureau, quoted at http://www.census.gov/popclock/, 11 May 2013

xxvi Tony Robbins, Personal Power II, Day 6 – The Driving Force

xxvii Tony Robbins, Personal Power II, Day 6 – The Driving Force

xxviii Ned Herrmann, The Whole Brain Business Book (New York: McGraw-Hill), 1996

xxix United States Census Bureau, quoted at http://www.census.gov/popclock/, 11 May 2013

xxx Charles W. Christian, 10 Rules of Respect, quoted at http://www.christianitytoday.com/le/1999/summer/9l3055.html, 11 May 2013

xxxi BusinessWeek, Commentary: Goodbye to an Ethicist, quoted at http://www.businessweek.com/stories/2003-02-09/commentary-goodbye-to-an-ethicist 11 May 2013

xxxii Fortune Magazine, CNN Money, 100 Best Companies to Work For, quoted at http://money.cnn.com/magazines/fortune/best-companies/2013/snapshots/94.html?iid=bc_fl_list, 11 May 2013

xxxiii J.C. Penney, Fifty Years with the Golden Rule (New York: Harper and Brothers, 1950), 16.

xxxiv Norman Beasley, Main Street Merchant (New York: Bantam, 1950), 63.

xxxv J.C. Penney, Fifty Years with the Golden Rule (New York: Harper and Brothers, 1950), 52.

xxxvi J.C. Penney, Fifty Years with the Golden Rule (New York: Harper and Brothers, 1950), 52.

xxxvii Government Executive, Study: Ethical breaches becoming common in government, quoted at http://www.govexec.com/pay-benefits/2008/01/study-ethical-breaches-becoming-common-in-government/26192/, 11 May 2013

xxxviii US Debt Clock.org, quoted at www.USDEBTCLOCK.org on 11 May 2013

xxxix C.S. Lewis, Mere Christianity (San Francisco: Harper San Francisco, 2001), 122.

xl Industry Week, People Who Cheat At Golf Cheat In Business, quoted at http://www.industryweek.com/corporate-culture/people-who-cheat-golf-cheat-business, 11 May 2013

xli Jack Welch, quoted at http://en.wikipedia.org/wiki/Jack_Welch 11 May 2013

xlii Pactolus, quoted at http://www.mythweb.com/encyc/entries/pactolus.html 11 May 2013

xliii United States Census Bureau, quoted at http://www.census.gov/popclock/, 11 May 2013

xliv Jamaica national bobsled team, quoted at http://en.wikipedia.org/wiki/Jamaica_national_bobsled_team 11 May 2013

xlv USA Today, WorldCom's whistle-blower tells her story, quoted at http://usatoday30.usatoday.com/money/companies/regulation/2008-02-14-cynthia-cooper-whistleblower_N.htm 11 May 2013

xlvi Forbes.com, The Nine Financiers, a Parable About Power, quoted at http://www.forbes.com/sites/joshuabrown/2012/07/25/the-nine-financiers-a-parable-about-power/ 11 May 2013

xlvii Mary Kay Ash Biography, quoted at http://www.biography.com/people/mary-kay-ash-197044 11 May 2013

xlviii Direct Selling Women's Alliance, quoted at www.dswa.org 11 May 2013

xlix WFDSA History, quoted at http://www.wfdsa.org/about_wfdsa/?fa=history 11 May 2013

l WFDSA Mission, quoted at http://www.wfdsa.org/about_wfdsa/?fa=mission 11 May 2013

li WFDSA Objectives, quoted at http://www.wfdsa.org/about_wfdsa/?fa=objectives 11 May 2013

lii Introduction to the WFDSA Code of Ethics, quoted at http://www.wfdsa.org/world_codes/about-the-code/ 11 May 2013

liii WFDSA Resources for DSAs and Member Companies, quoted at http://www.wfdsa.org/world_codes/resources-member-companies/ 11 May 2013

liv WFDSA Information for Direct Sellers, quoted at http://www.wfdsa.org/world_codes/information-direct-sellers/ 11 May 2013

lv WFDSA Information for Consumers, quoted at http://www.wfdsa.org/world_codes/information-consumers/ 11 May 2013

lvi WFDSA Code of Ethics Recognition Program, quoted at http://www.wfdsa.org/world_codes/code-of-ethics-recognition-program/ 11 May 2013

lvii WFDSA Code of Ethics, quoted at http://www.wfdsa.org/files/world-codes/code-book.pdf 11 May 2013

lviii Direct Selling Association, quoted at http://www.dsa.org/ 11 May 2013

lix DirectSelling411.com, quoted at http://www.directselling411.com/ 11 May 2013

lx Direct Selling Association, Understanding the DSA Code of Ethics, quoted at http://www.dsa.org/ethics/understanding-code/ 11 May 2013

lxi Direct Selling Association, The Code and Member Companies, quoted at http://www.dsa.org/ethics/member-companies/ 11 May 2013

lxii Direct Selling Association, The Code and Direct Sellers, quoted at http://www.dsa.org/ethics/direct-sellers/ 11 May 2013

lxiii Direct Selling Association, The Code and Consumers, quoted at http://www.dsa.org/ethics/consumers/ 11 May 2013

lxiv Direct Selling Association, Code Responsibility Officers, quoted at http://www.dsa.org/ethics/cro/ 11 May 2013

lxv Direct Selling Association, Worldwide Obligations, quoted at http://www.dsa.org/ethics/worldwide-obligations/ 11 May 2013

lxvi Direct Selling Association, Code of Ethics in Action, quoted at http://www.dsa.org/ethics/in-action/ 11 May 2013

lxvii Direct Selling Association, Filing a Code Complaint, quoted at http://www.dsa.org/ethics/complaint/ 11 May 2013

lxviii Direct Selling Association, The Facts About Direct Selling that you Won't Hear from Short Sellers, quoted at http://www.dsa.org/ethics/?fa=facts2 11 May 2013

lxix Direct Selling Association, The Facts about Internal Consumption, quoted at http://www.dsa.org/ethics/internalconsumptionfacts.pdf 11 May 2013

lxx Direct Selling Association, Code of Ethics, quoted at http://www.dsa.org/ethics/code/code1211.pdf 11 May 2013

lxxi Direct Sellers Association, The Association, quoted at http://dsa.ca/content/association/ Sept 8, 2013

lxxii Direct Sellers Association, Consumer Protection quoted at http://dsa.ca/content/consumerprotection/ Sept 8, 2013

lxxiii Direct Sellers Association, Code of Ethics, quoted at http://dsa.ca/content/consumerprotection/codeofethics.php Sept 8, 2013

lxxiv Direct Sellers Association, DSA's Commitment, quoted at http://dsa.ca/content/consumerprotection/commitment.php Sept 8, 2013

lxxv Direct Sellers Association, Recognizing Reputable Firms, quoted at
http://dsa.ca/content/consumerprotection/recognizing.php Sept 8, 2013

lxxvi Direct Sellers Association, Complaint Resolution, quoted at
http://dsa.ca/content/consumerprotection/complaint.php Sept 8, 2013

lxxvii Direct Sellers Association, Government Relations, quoted at
http://dsa.ca/content/govtrelations/ Sept 8, 2013

lxxviii House of Commons Canada, Bill C-51, An Act to amend the Food and
Drugs Act and to make consequential amendments to other Acts, quoted at
http://www.dsa.ca/fileBin/mediaLibrary/C-51_1.pdf

lxxix Direct Sellers Association, Issues Advocacy, quoted at
http://dsa.ca/content/govtrelations/issues.php Sept 8, 2013